Marine Advisors
With the Vietnamese Marine Corps

Selected Documents prepared by the U.S. Marine Advisory Unit,
Naval Advisory Group

Compiled and Edited by
Charles D. Melson and Wanda J. Renfrow

Occasional Paper

HISTORY DIVISION
MARINE CORPS UNIVERSITY
QUANTICO, VIRGINIA

2009

Other Publications in the Occasional Papers Series

Vietnam Histories Workshop: Plenary Session. Jack Shulimson, editor. 9 May1983. 31 pp.

Vietnam Revisited; Conversation with William D. Broyles, Jr. Colonel John G. Miller, USMC, editor. 11 December 1984. 48 pp.

Bibliography on Khe Sanh USMC Participation. Commander Ray W. Strubbe, CHC, USNR (Ret), compiler. April 1985. 54 pp.

Alligators, Buffaloes, and Bushmasters: The History of the Development of the LVT Through World War II. Major Alfred Dunlop Bailey, USMC (Ret). 1986. 272 pp.

Leadership Lessons and Remembrances from Vietnam. Lieutenant General Herman Nickerson, Jr., USMC (Ret). 1988. 93 pp.

The Problems of U.S. Marine Corps Prisoners of War in Korea. James Angus MacDonald, Jr. 1988. 295 pp.

John Archer Lejeune, 1869-1942, Register of His Personal Papers. Lieutenant Colonel Merrill L. Bartlett, USMC (Ret). 1988. 123 pp.

To Wake Island and Beyond: Reminiscences. Brigadier General Woodrow M. Kessler, USMC (Ret). 1988. 145 pp.

Thomas Holcomb, 1879-1965, Register of His Personal Papers. Gibson B. Smith. 1988. 229 pp.

Curriculum Evolution, Marine Corps Command and Staff College, 1920-1988. Lieutenant Colonel Donald F. Bittner, USMCR. 1988. 112 pp.

Herringbone Cloak-GI Dagger, Marines of the OSS. Major Robert E. Mattingly, USMC. 1989. 315 pp.

The Journals of Marine Second Lieutenant Henry Bulls Watson, 1845-1848. Charles R. Smith, editor. 1990. 420 pp.

When the Russians Blinked: The U.S. Maritime Response to the Cuban Missile Crisis. Major John M. Young, USMCR. 1990. 246 pp.

Marines in the Mexican War. Gabrielle M. Neufeld Santelli. Edited by Charles R. Smith. 1991. 63 pp.

The Development of Amphibious Tactics in the U.S. Navy. General Holland M. Smith, USMC (Ret). 1992. 89 pp.

James Guthrie Harbord, 1866-1947, Register of His Personal Papers. Lieutenant Colonel Merrill L. Bartlett, USMC. 1995. 47 pp.

The Impact of Project 100,000 on the Marine Corps. Captain David A. Dawson, USMC. 1995. 247 pp.

Marine Corps Aircraft: 1913-2000. Major John M. Elliot, USMC (Ret). 2002. 126 pp.

Thomas Holcomb and the Advent of the Marine Corps Defense Battalion, 1936-1941. David J. Ulbrich. 2004. 78 pp.

Marine History Operations in Iraq, Operation Iraq Freedom I, A Catalog of Interviews and Recordings. Lieutenant Colonel Nathan S. Lowrey, USMCR. 2005. 254 pp.

With the 1st Marine Division in Iraq, 2003. No Greater Friend, No Worse Enemy. Lieutenant Colonel Michael S. Groen, USMC. 2006. 413 pp.

Marine Advisors: With the Vietnamese Provincial Reconnaissance Units, 1966-1970. Colonel Andrew R. Finlayson, USMC (Ret). 2009. 72 pp.

Operation Millpond: U.S. Marines in Thailand, 1961. Colonel George R. Hofmann, Jr., USMC (Ret). 2009. 36 pp.

Foreword

The History Division has undertaken the publication for limited distribution of various studies, theses, compilations, bibliographies, monographs, and memoirs, as well as proceedings at selected workshops, seminars, symposia, and similar colloquia, which it considers to be of significant value for audiences interested in Marine Corps history. These "Occasional Papers," which are chosen for their intrinsic worth, must reflect structured research, present a contribution to historical knowledge not readily available in published sources, and reflect original content on the part of the author, compiler, or editor. It is the intent of the division that these occasional papers be distributed to select institutions such as service schools, official Department of Defense historical agencies, and directly concerned Marine Corps organizations, so the information contained therein will be available for study and exploitation.

Dr. Charles P. Neimeyer
Director of Marine Corps History

Preface

I first served with Vietnamese Marines in 1972 when they came on board the U.S. Navy ships that Battalion Landing Team 1/9 was embarked on. They were preparing for an amphibious landing to counter the North Vietnamese Army's Spring Offensive in Military Region 1 (I Corps) in South Vietnam. They brought with them their U.S. Marine advisors who were known by the senior members of the battalion. We had already witnessed or heard of the exploits of then-Captain John Ripley and Lieutenant Colonel Gerry Turley in blunting the initial attacks of the Easter Offensive. As the Vietnamese were formed into helicopter or boat teams and fed a meal before going ashore, they bantered with the American Marines and Sailors, telling them to come along to "kill communists."

After a turbulent start to the offensive, the Vietnamese Marines exhibited the fighting spirit that elite units create for themselves. This was reflected in the various names of their battalions that were the focus of their unit identification. The infantry battalions had a series of nicknames and slogans that were reflected on their unit insignia: 1st Battalion's "Wild Bird," 2d Battalion's "Crazy Buffalo," 3d Battalion's "Sea Wolf," 4th Battalion's "Killer Shark," 5th Battalion's "Black Dragon," 6th Battalion's "Sacred Bird," 7th Battalion's "Black Tiger," 8th Battalion's "Sea Eagle," and 9th Battalion's "Mighty Tiger." For the artillery units, this was the 1st Battalion's "Lightning Fire," 2d Battalion's "Sacred Arrow," and 3d Battalion's "Sacred Bow." Support and service battalions followed this example as well.

The 9th Marine Amphibious Brigade and its embarked troops provided helicopters, amphibious tractors, and landing craft support for a series of attacks leading to the recapture of Quang Tri City through the fall of 1972. In addition, command and control facilities and liaison were provided to the Republic of Vietnam's I Corps and Military Advisory Command Vietnam's 1st Regional Advisory Command in the sustained counteroffensive. This reinforced the impression made by the Vietnamese Marines themselves. This began my interest in the story that follows.

The period after World War II saw a number of associated Marine Corps formed in the republics of China, Korea, Vietnam, the Philippines, Indonesia, and Thailand. They had been founded, with the help of foreign military aid, to fight the various conflicts to contain communist expansion in the region. Also present at various times were other Marines from the Netherlands, France, and Great Britain. The beginnings of the Cold War witnessed this proliferation of amphibious forces in Asia, in part because of the reputation the U.S. Marines had earned in the cross Pacific drive against Japan and in other postwar confrontations. This is about one of them, the Vietnamese Marine Corps or *Thuy Quan Luc Chien* (*TQLC*).

This occasional paper provides documents on the topics of the Vietnamese Marines and the U.S. Marine Advisory Unit from this period. William D. Wischmeyer created the reference that the unit and history was based on. As a captain, he drafted the "Vietnamese Marine Corps/Marine Advisory Unit Historical Summary, 1954-1973," signed off by the senior Marine advisor on 22 March 1973. Another valuable collection of Vietnamese Marine Corps material was kept by then-Lieutenant Colonel Anthony Lukeman when the Vietnamese Marine Corps Logistics Support Branch, Navy Division, Defense Attaché Office was closed in 1975. It and the other essential source material enclosed were sent as part of the Marine Advisory Unit's command chronology, in the Gray Research Center archive, Quantico, Virginia.

Ms. Wanda J. Renfrow took a mix of 40-year-old documents and electronic copies and made them a coherent whole. They were edited for clarity and continuity. Thanks go to Virginia Tech intern Mary E. Dail for providing the oral history list, to the U.S. Marine Corps Advisor's Association, and Master Sergeant (Ret) Daniel K. Whitton for continued interest and support. I also acknowledge the efforts of Kenneth H. Williams for editorial guidance, and William S. Hill for design and layout.

Charles D. Melson
Chief Historian
U.S. Marine Corps History Division

Table of Contents

Foreword 3

Preface 5

The Vietnamese Marine Corps, 1954-1975 9

Senior U.S. Marine Advisors, 1954-1975 15

Document: SAB [Senior Advisor Brief] Helpful Hints 17

Document: What You Should Know When Assigned to a Vietnamese Marine Battalion as an Advisor 19

Document: Techniques of Advising 25

Document: Standing Operation Procedures for Marine Advisory Unit 29

U.S. Marine Advisors to the Vietnamese Marine Corps, 1954-1975 175

Further Reading 181

Oral Histories 185

The Vietnamese Marine Corps, 1954-1975

Three Corps fought together in Vietnam from 1965 through 1973. Each of these was a similar formation, but with its own history and traditions: the United States Marines, the Vietnamese Marines, and the Korean Marines. Common to each was a reputation for toughness on themselves and any enemy, strong unit pride, and loyalty with a privileged place within the defense structure of their respective countries. This is the story of one of them.

When the French departed Indochina, they left behind the fledgling armed forces of the Vietnamese republic. Included were the riverine forces of the navy and an assortment of army commandos that had provided the troops for them. These had formed the river assault divisions (*Dinassauts*) that Dr. Bernard B. Fall observed as "one of a few worthwhile contributions" to military tactics of the First Indochina War (1945-1954). After the Geneva Agreement that arranged the withdrawal of France from Indochina and the partition of Vietnam into north and south pending elections, the Americans moved to help the government of South Vietnam against the communist bloc-supported People's Republic of Vietnam. The commandos were formed into two battalions and grouped at Nha Trang when the separation of Vietnam into north and south was completed.

On 1 October 1954, the mixed commando units were designated as the Marine Infantry of the Vietnamese Navy. In April 1956, it became known as the Vietnamese Marine Corps of the Navy, consisting of a Marine Group of two landing battalions. By 1960, the date on Vietnam's Campaign Medal, a state of armed conflict existed between the two Vietnams and their allies in the Second Indochina War (1960-1975). This was a civil war that had international connotations between several world powers and their clients. It was a confrontation that displayed a full spectrum of violence, from individual terrorist acts and guerrilla fighting to conventional land combat, with extensive sea and air components. Enemy forces ranged from National Liberation Front guerrillas in South Vietnam, of varying quality and quantity, to the regulars of the People's Army of Vietnam, who infiltrated into South Vietnam along the Ho Chi Minh Trail. They also defended North Vietnam with conventional forces. In 1961, the Vietnamese Marines became part of the Republic of South Vietnam's armed forces general reserve. Expansion resulted from successful employment against dissidents and bandits, which led to the formation of a 5,000-man Marine brigade in 1962. Vietnamese Marine Corps influence increased in part with the role it played in complex national politics that saw marines involved in coups in 1960, 1963, and 1964. This continual balancing of power was reflected in assignment of forces, commanders, and the direction of the war.

The formation of its own training and replacement centers allowed the Vietnamese Marines to keep up to strength without relying on the army for manpower. Both officers and men attended schools in the United States at Quantico, Virginia, where a generation of Vietnamese and Americans met and served together. One Vietnamese Marine commandant, General Le Nguyen Khang, observed that his men were proud "to be associated in spirit and deed with the select group of professional military men of many nations who call themselves Marines."

Of the total of 565,350 South Vietnamese in the armed forces in 1965, more than 6,500 were Marines. In 1965, the Vietnamese Marine Brigade was organized into a corps headquarters, two task force headquarters ("A" and "B"), five infantry battalions, an artillery battalion, and supporting units of engineers, motor transport, military police, medical, and reconnaissance. Headquarters were located in Saigon, with outlying facilities at Song Than, Thu Duc, and Vung Tau. A colonel, who was dual-hatted as a service and the brigade com-

Vietnamese Marine Division, 1972

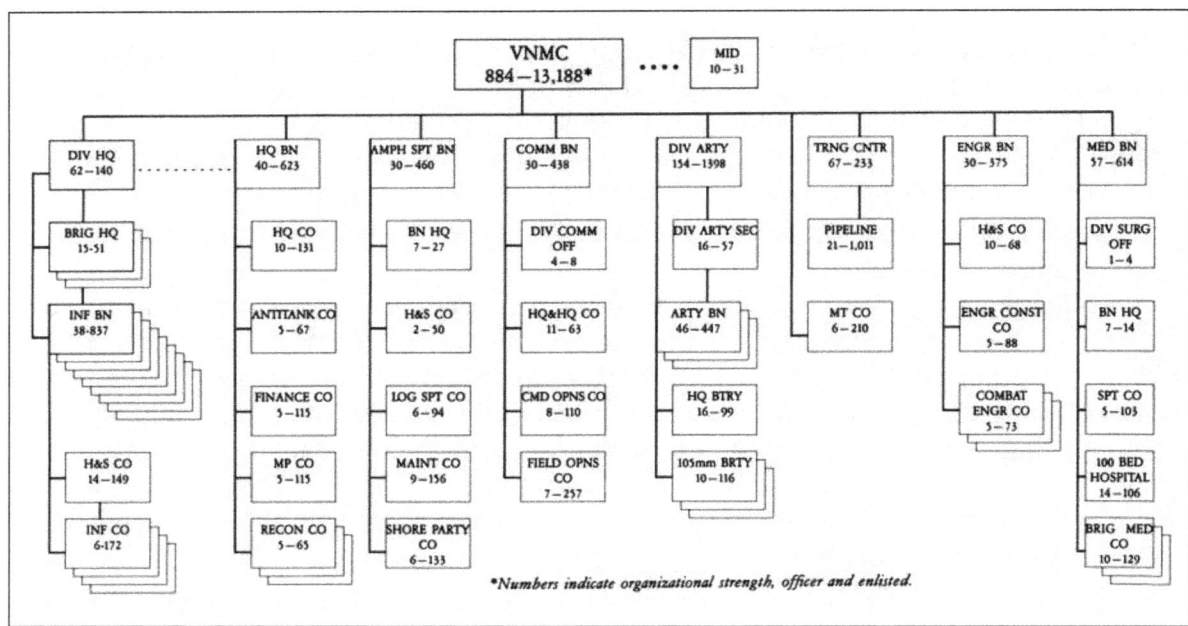

Adapted from Marine Advisory Unit Material

mander, led it. By this time, Vietnamese Marines were separated from the Vietnamese Navy and answerable to the high command of the Republic of Vietnam Armed Forces. Present was a 28-man advisory unit from the U.S. Marine Corps. American field advisors were down to the battalion level.

By 1966, the Marines formed another battalion and realigned supporting units to become a more balanced combined arms force. It was still lacking in armor, aircraft, and logistic support. In 1968, a Marine division was formed of two brigades. In 1970, there were three brigades, nine infantry battalions, and three artillery battalions. Supporting units continued to be formed through the following year, reaching a peak of 939 officers and 14,290 men at the time the Americans withdrew. This figure expanded to more than 15,000 men in 1973. Total casualty figures are not available, but in the heavy 1972 fighting, some 2,455 Marines were killed in action and another 7,840 men were wounded during the same period. To face the military crisis in 1975, three additional battalions and a fourth brigade were formed before the South Vietnamese defeat.

The Southeast Asia theater of operations was divided into North Vietnam, South Vietnam, the Tonkin Gulf littoral, and the inland frontiers of Laos and Cambodia. The country of South Vietnam consisted of political provinces grouped together into military regions or tactical zones numbered from I through IV, from north to the south. The country was divided geographically from east to west into a coastal plain, a piedmont region, and the central highlands.

As part of the national reserve, the Vietnamese Marines found themselves from the 17th Parallel in the north to the islands of the extreme south. When assigned to a specific corps area, the Marines would serve under Army of the Republic of Vietnam (ARVN) general officers, and the corps commanders. Prior to 1965, most operations were by single battalions in III and IV Corps. A variety of counterinsurgency operations were engaged in, to include search and destroy, search and clear, helicopter and riverine assault, and security tasks. Characteristic employment was in response to critical situations requiring rapid movement with short notice

After 1965, the Marines deployed more to the I and II Corps areas as the war progressed away from the Delta and capital regions. Multiple battalion operations became the norm through the use of task force headquarters. Two battalions under Task Force A concluded a series of operations over a four-month period that resulted in 444 communists killed and another 150 taken prisoner. This included a notable engagement in April 1965 near An Thai, Binh Dinh Province, which resulted in the 2d Infantry Battalion earning a U.S. Presidential Unit Citation for a successful defense against a superior communist force.

From 1966 through 1967, the Marines spent more time in I Corps and conducted operations in conjunction with the Americans in this critical locale. It was observed that Vietnamese Marines were in the field 75 percent of the time, then the highest figure obtained by South Vietnamese forces. During the 1968 Tet Offensive, the Marines fought in both Saigon and Hue to defeat the communist attempt at a general uprising. During this year, the Vietnamese Marines maintained a casualty to kill ratio of one to seven.

In March 1969, the 5th Infantry Battalion earned a U.S. Navy Unit Commendation for action in III Corps, near Bien Hoa. This resulted in 73 communists killed, 20 taken prisoners, and captured weapons. Vietnamese Marines took part in the aggressive South Vietnamese external operations that coincided with the American departure: Cambodia in 1970 and Laos in 1971. The Laotian incursion was the first time a division command post took the field to control maneuver brigades.

By 1971, at least two Vietnamese Marine brigades remained in I Corps facing the demilitarized zone and the North Vietnamese, filling the vacuum left when the Americans moved from this region. During the Spring Offensive in 1972, the Vietnamese Marines were fully employed for the defense of the north and at first were used piecemeal under control of the 3d ARVN Division. The Marine Division established itself as a major fighting force in the month-long battle to recapture Quang Tri City; in the process, the Vietnamese Marines killed an estimated 17,819 North Vietnamese soldiers, took 156 prisoners, and captured more than 5,000 weapons and vehicles. At the beginning of 1973, the Marine Division was regarded by the South Vietnamese as an "outstanding unit" of the Republic of Vietnam Armed Forces.

The Vietnamese Marines remained committed to the defense of the Demilitarized Zone through 1974. First ordered to protect Hue and Da Nang from the communist attack in spring 1975, the Marines were hastily withdrawn with the collapse of the South Vietnamese in the northern provinces. Five battalion commanders and some 40 company commanders were killed during the fighting. The division reorganized and deployed its remaining forces at Long Binh for the final battle for Saigon. There it stayed through the subsequent fighting at the end of April 1975. At that point, the Vietnamese Marine Corps ceased to exist except in memory and history. For the Vietnamese, the conflict was the end of a 30-year war in which the Vietnamese Marine Corps played a part until the bitter end.

The Development of the U.S. Marine Advisory Unit in Vietnam, 1955-1973

With this background on the Vietnamese Marines, a look at the U.S. Marine Corps advisory effort is in order. From the time it was established in 1955 until 1961, this unit consisted of a lieutenant colonel and two captains serving as the senior Marine advisor and assistant Marine advisors of the Marine Advisory Division of the Navy Section of the Military Assistance and Advisory Group, Vietnam. In December 1961, the organization of the advisory division was

Marine Advisory Unit, 1972

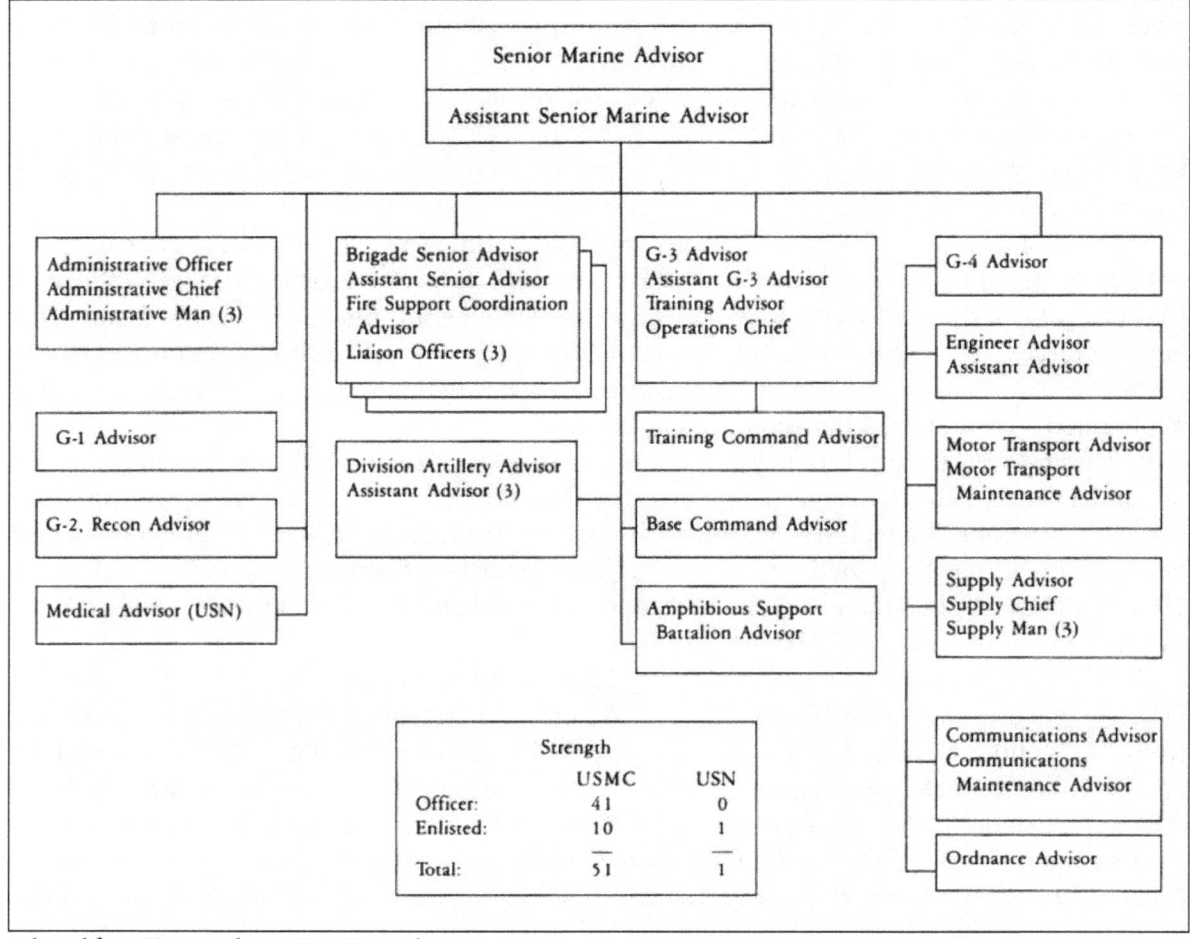

Adapted from Marine Advisory Unit Material

expanded to include battalion-level "field" advisors for the infantry and artillery units. This provided an overall strength of 8 officers and 16 enlisted Marines, including a senior and assistant senior advisor (lieutenant colonel and major), an administrative element, a logistics element, an enlisted small unit training advisor (gunnery sergeant), four officers and enlisted infantry advisors (captains and staff sergeants), and an officer and enlisted artillery advisor (major and gunnery sergeant). By 1963, an additional small unit training advisor was added, but the enlisted field advisors were eliminated.

In May 1964, the division was transferred to the Military Assistance Command, Vietnam and became the Marine Advisory Unit, Naval Advisory Group as part of an overall restructuring of American support. That year it increased in strength to 20 officers and 11 enlisted men. By January 1965, the requirement for more officer advisors resulted in another restructuring and a new strength of 25 officers, 2 Marines, and 1 Navy Corpsman. The senior Marine was now a colonel in keeping with the rank of the Vietnamese commandant.

The mission continued to evolve along with the growth and expansion of the Vietnamese Marine Corps. The principle effort was directed at tactical advice and assistance, but staff and logistical advisors played a key role as these tasks took on greater importance in Vietnamese functions. Between January 1968 and March 1969, the Marine Advisory Unit expanded from 28 officers and 5 enlisted (including a Navy medical officer and corpsman) to 49 officers and 10 enlisted. In addition to a small administrative support office, there were now G-1, 2, 3, 4, communications and medical advisory elements. Field advisory teams existed at the brigade and battalion level (majors and captains). It should be also noted that by this time in the war, a stream of Vietnamese Marine officers and staff noncommissioned officer had attended U.S. Marine Corps schools and training course in the United States. American military assistance programs saw to a steady supply and upgrading of weapons and equipment. In 1971, a U.S. Navy Unit Commendation recognized this effort.

It was in March 1972 that the Marine Advisory Unit reached peak strength of 67. By this time, the advisory effort focused primarily on training, logistics, and staff functions. In keeping with the reduction of "Free World Military Forces" in South Vietnam, the advisory unit was concurrently being reduced and field advisors were withdrawn from the battalions to brigade-level. The Easter Offensive changed these plans, and the advisory unit fully deployed its then 52 advisors to the field in support of the Vietnamese Marine Division in May. As continued combat exhaustion and illness depleted this staff, in July 1972 an additional nine U.S. Marine advisors were provided as augmentation (nine more would arrive by year's end). In addition, there was increased direct support from Sub Unit 1, 1st Air-Naval Gunfire Company (USMC), the 20th Tactical Air Support Squadron (USAF), and 14th Company, 1st Signal Brigade (USA). This American support, and that of "a few Marines," contributed to the Vietnamese Marines defining victory at Quang Tri City in 1972.

The last Senior Marine Advisor, Colonel Joshua W. Dorsey III, concluded that the "advisory program initially was designed to improve the expertise of the tactical unit commander. The success of this program enabled the Marine Advisory Unit to reorient its efforts so that by early 1972, permanent battalion advisors were no longer required. At that point in time, liaison officers were provided to battalions on an as required basis for coordination of U.S. supporting arms and emphasis was primarily directed towards brigade and division level advice and assistance as well as technical management guidance in logistical and administrative fields. By the time of the withdrawal of the Marine Advisory Unit, the Marine Division was almost totally self-sufficient in all other areas."

With the cease-fire and withdrawal of American forces from South Vietnam in 1973, Marine Advisory Unit logistical and advisory functions were turned over to the Vietnamese Marine Corps Logistics Support Branch of the Navy Division of the Defense Attaché Office. This marked the end of an era of advisory efforts to the Vietnamese Marines.

Senior U.S. Marine Advisors, 1954-1973

LtCol Victor J. Croziat	August 54–June 56
LtCol William N. Wilkes	June 56–June 58
LtCol Frank R. Wilkinson Jr.	June 58–June 60
LtCol Clifford J. Robichaud Jr.	June 60–August 61
LtCol Robert E. Brown	August 61–October 62
LtCol Clarence G. Moody Jr.	October 62–October 63
Col Wesley C. Noren	October 63–September 64
Col William P. Nesbit	September 64–July 65
Col John A. MacNeil	July 65–July 66
Col Nels E. Anderson	July 66–July 67
Col Richard L. Michael Jr.	July 67–July 68
Col Leroy V. Corbett	July 68–July 69
Col William M. VanZuyen	July 69–June 70
LtCol Alexander P. McMillan	June 70–July 70
Col Francis W. Tief	July 70–July 71
Col Joshua W. Dorsey III	July 71–March 73

Chief, Vietnamese Marine Corps Logistics Support Branch, 1973-1975

LtCol Walter D. Fillmore	March 73–June 73
LtCol George E. Strickland	June 73–June 74
LtCol Anthony Lukeman	June 74–April 75

SAB [Senior Advisor Brief]

Helpful Hints

Travel

All the advisors going to a Marine Advisory Unit will fly directly to Saigon from Travis Air Force Base in California. When they get into the commercial airport at San Francisco it takes about an hour and a half to get to Travis. The fare is about $2.50. If you go by cab it is 26.00. I'd advise going by the bus. Bachelor officers quarter rooms are available at Travis if you should happen to arrive there early. The cost runs about $1.50 to $2.50. It has a real good Officers Club–opens 24 hours a day–real good chow, and 4 or 5 bars.

Once you get to Travis you will check in with the Marine Liaison. The flight to Saigon takes a total of 22 hours depending on what route you go. If you go the northern route you'll land at Anchorage, Alaska then down into Japan and straight to Saigon. When you arrive at Saigon - the advisors going to the Vietnamese Marines will usually be met by the Senior Marine Advisor or the Assistant Senior Marine Advisor. All advisors will report into Koepler Compound. This is a U.S. Army affair that consists of 3 or 4 days of general briefing security briefings and things of this nature. Once you're finished at Koepler Compound you will then go to the Marine Advisory Unit where you'll be issued all your field gear and be given briefing there generally on the organization of the Vietnamese Marine Corps of the Advisory Unit itself and things of this nature. Also this is where you will get your assignment either as a Battalion Advisor or Task Force Advisor. The ones specifically designated for staff advisors, engineer advisors, supply advisors, administrative advisors, and the S-3 advisor will stay in Saigon the majority of the time. All advisors at the Marine Advisory Unit are assigned permanent bachelor officers quarter rooms in Saigon. The majority have closed messes that are available. They are run by the Army again and have bars. The field advisor will spend 80 or 90% of their time on operations any place in III and IV Corps areas.

Gear

Travel as light as possible. Military gear, two sets of cotton khaki uniforms, short sleeve shirts. Your summer service "Alpha" traveling over from San Francisco, dress shoes, couple pair of socks, at least 6 sets of skivvies (green) six pairs of wool socks, couple web belts and buckles and 2 utility caps and a couple utility uniforms. Civilian gear, all wash and wear. One wash and wear suit-maybe two pair trousers, couple of short sleeve white shirts, couple sport shirts, also take a tie and other related gear, socks and of course your toilet gear. Definitely no sense taking any "782" gear or personal weapons, everything you need is available in Vietnam. As far as weapons are concerned you can be armed with a M16, and .45, to an AK47 and a RPG7. You will be issued 4 sets of camouflage equipment as we call them "Tiger Suits". You will have to buy a rain hat-these are made out of the same camouflage material. They generally run about 200 piasters. Also a green beret which is about 600 piasters. A Vietnamese hammock which is about 500 piasters and name tags, patches and different paraphernalia that you put on your tiger suits. When you get into Saigon I'd really recommend opening a checking account at the Bank of America or Chase Manhattan of New York. There's a real good deal on this–there's no service charge on your checking account. All of your checks are free and besides that you're paid 5% on your minimum quarterly balance. The nice thing is you can retain this account when you get back to the states. The same thing applies-checks are free and you get your 5% interest. They've got a real fine Post Exchange in Saigon. They have good stereo gear-the only problem is that it goes real fast.

Operations

On operations I'd take a couple sets of utilities, couple pair of socks, a Marine hat, poncho, poncho liner, your hammock and maybe your air mattress depending on the area you're going to operate. Definitely take instant coffee, toilet articles, flashlight, couple extra batteries, salt tablets and halazone tablets and anti-diarrhea pills. For the base camp area you ought to take along a couple extra sets of skivvies, soap, canned chow, radio, cot, air mattress, reading and writing gear and check book. As far as the money goes, the advisors over there can help you out on this–a lot depends on the length of deployment. Normally about 30 bucks military payment certificate and about 30 dollars in piasters. You will be paying your counterpart for your chow. You will strictly be eating Vietnamese food when you're out on an operation. This runs about 50 piasters a day-13 bucks a month. For this you can get all the rice and nuc mam you can eat plus all the assorted goodies. You will be eating with chopsticks-practice. The current table of organization of the Marine Advisory Unit is 27 officers, 4 enlisted men. These enlisted folks are back in Saigon. They operate on the staff. When you're with the infantry battalion, the senior advisor is going to have three Vietnamese working for him, a driver, a cowboy, and a radio operator. The assistant advisor will have a cowboy, and a radio operator. This cowboy carries your pack for you; makes your coffee in the morning; makes you a sleeping place, and guards your gear. Generally he is an all around handy-man. Your radio operator-about the only function he performs is carrying your radio.

What You Should Know When Assigned To A Vietnamese Marine Battalion As An Advisor

If you have received orders assigning you to a Vietnamese Marine Battalion as an advisor, undoubtedly many questions will come to your mind: "What will I do?", "What should I know about the Vietnamese people and their war?", "How do Vietnamese Marines fight?"

We consider an advisor as a new "bride" because he knows what he is supposed to do, but he may probably have some difficulty in doing it.

The following information does not intend to teach you "the role of the advisor," yet, it reflects some basic ideas which may help you to perform your duty easier and most likely lead to a more enjoyable tour.

Organization of the Vietnamese Marine Corps

The Vietnamese Marine Corps was originally established in 1954 and comprised several river groups, a number of ranger companies and commands units, which had been operating as part of the French Union Forces. By early 1955, the Vietnamese Marine Corps expanded from an initial strength of 1,200 to 1,800 members and consisted of two infantry battalions and a headquarter and service company. Its organization resembled the USMC in weapons and structure. By 1959, the VNMC had added a headquarters group, a 3rd Infantry Battalion and a 4.2-inch Mortar Company. By 1960 and 1961 a medical company, a 75mm Howitzer Battery and another infantry battalion were formed. Continuing its expansions the VNMC had added an amphibious support battalion and a 105mm Howitzer Battery. It has grown now to six infantry battalions, an artillery battalion, and an amphibious support battalion.

The inherent mission of the Vietnamese Marine brigade is: "to conduct amphibious operations, and to assist the counterinsurgent effort." However, along with the airborne division, and because of the tactical situation, the Vietnamese Marine brigade forms the general reserve force of the Republic of Vietnamese, and as such, is employed throughout the IV Corps areas, and accordingly involved in any movement that may be by air, land or sea on a short notice.

Vietnamese Customs and Politeness

— Despite their contacts and dealings with the western people for about a century, the Vietnamese still keep their customs and traditions, which are rooted in and conditioned mostly by religious belief and cultural environment.

— The Vietnamese family is based on the principle of unity of the paterfamilias authority and was strongly constituted due to the necessity of perpetuating the cult of ancestors. It never admits to the instrument of the public powers and constitutes a homogeneous unit in, which the father of the family performs the role of a chief, a priest and a magistrate.

— The Vietnamese are deeply motivated by their religions. As each family has its altar, each village has its temple or dinh for the worship of a tutelar god. Temples, pagodas, and churches or any religious places must be respected. The traditional family also has a deep respect for the dead, therefore, altars and graves must be considered as reverent sites.

— In speaking to people different terms are used to denote the hierarchic discrimination, respect, age, sex and family relationships.

— Vietnamese names are usually composed of three elements appearing in the following order: first, the family or clan name (*ho*); second, the middle name (*chulot* or cushion word); third; the given name (*ten*). The given name is not the same for every member of the family. The middle name, if there is one, nearly always tells the sex of the individual, therefore girls' names, most of the time have "*thi*" as the cushion. However, several family names have long been composed of two words and as such they have no middle name.

— Traditionally the Vietnamese woman, like any other Asian woman, relies on destiny to govern her life and future. They are not supposed to participate in any social or public organizations but to try solely to be a good "homewife," and loyal to their husband who "overshadows" them. However, today, these rules are not so rigorous and a woman is permitted to remarry and become a member of a social or public organization.

— The most important Vietnamese festival day is *Tet* or the New Year, which lasts the first three days of the first month of the lunar calendar. According to custom, on the first day, of Tet, children have to greet their parents first as do subordinates to their superiors. Greetings and wishes will generally concern good luck, prosperity, long life.

— The Vietnamese do not practice "Dutch Treat." The older or senior is expected to pick up the check even if he joined a friend by chance in a restaurant.

— Vietnamese rules of politeness are inspired by Confucianism. In olden times students of Confucian schools were taught politeness first, and then they were given the rest of their education. It was also prescribed that they respect first their emperor, second their teacher and third their father "*Quận-Su-Phu.*"

— Vietnamese politeness is quite delicate in the way of speaking, writing, or acting. Speaking of himself or anything he possesses, a man should qualify them as humble or poor while the person and everything owned by the person to whom he speaks or writes are nice and perfect.

— To express an idea or an opinion one would say "From my humble opinion, my poor thinking . . ." A person who is too polite to disagree directly with someone would say "May I ask your permission to tell you . . ."Then his interlocutor will say with modesty "I dare not, sir, please."

— However, today Vietnamese politeness is not so straight laced in some points of view such as greeting a guest. A person can shake hands instead of joining his hands on his breast and bending deeply at the waist. To greet each other, a man and woman would incline their heads lightly. In olden times a person would look down when talking to his parents or superiors to impart the meaning of not "staring" at people greater standing.

— Talking to an old man or superior with arms akimbo or hands in the trouser pockets or sitting with one ankle crossed on the opposite knee while visiting the host's house, are considered as impolite.

— A person will become angry if someone slaps him on his head or beckons to him with one finger, snapping his fingers or whistling, as the Vietnamese use such gestures only for animals. The proper, polite method of beckoning a Vietnamese is a movement of the wrist and hand similar to a wave or the arm and hand signal for squad.

With a Vietnamese Marine Battalion

— As many questions came to your mind before you joined the Vietnamese Marine battalion, your counterpart also has many questions too: "Who is this new guy?" "Will he harass me with scattershot suggestion?" "What does he know about the Vietnam War and Vietnamese 'Sea-Tigers'?" "How much is he going to help me?" Since the advisor will remain almost permanently with his counterpart, he needs to understand him and his unit not only physically but also morally and psychologically. Another important point that should be emphasized is that the advisors ability will be judged in the first battle he and his counterpart participate in and depending on the efficiency of the advice will be the trust place in him.

— When you arrive at the battalion, the Headquarters and Service Company commander will introduce you to three "good fellows" who will stay with you and help you during your work with the battalion: your "cowboy," your radio-operator and your driver. Your cowboy! He is a good, strong Marine who will help you with small services, and during any fighting he will be your bodyguard. During operations, since you are busy, he will help you carry your gear and five days of food, plus his own. It is too heavy, isn't it? Therefore, he will appreciate it if such things as cameras, romance books, Maxwell bottles and transistor radios will be carried by yourself as long as you want to enjoy such facilities during an operation.

— As I have mentioned previously, the Vietnamese Marine Corps, as a general reserve force, may be involved anywhere throughout the IV Corps area. A Marine task force can be attached to any corps or Army division as the main attacking force or reaction force depending on the enemy situation.

— If you work in I or II Corps area, you may have chance to climb high mountains with thick vegetation, where, in the dry season, the water problem is more concerning that the enemy. In the rainy season the water level rises considerably and currents become tremendously strong–You can send a squad patrol across a stream and a couple of hours later, this squad, on returning, will find the same stream turned into a raging river.

— In the III Corps you may become familiar with the *Rungsat*, a wet and sticky, muddy area, covered with heavy mangroves and laced by innumerable streams many of that are not shown in your map. Here you will be interested in the "*Dong-Nai*" boats, which are suited for this kind of terrain.

— If you work in the IV Corps, you may be landed in "*U-Minh*" forest, an inundated and muddy terrain with thick vegetation where the water, red and dirty, rises permanently about your waist, and you will have no chance to see the sun except as a weak and indistinct light that is what "*U-Minh*" means. Do not forget to bring your hammock if you want to relax at night and prevent hundreds of mosquitoes from boring you.

— During the fighting sometimes the advisor and his counterpart do not get a chance to talk to each other, except for some tactical change or decision, since the counterpart is busy with his companies and the advisor has to adjust U.S. air strikes or artillery fire. The battalion's S-3 will moderate the coordination by informing both his company and the advisor of all necessary information and suggestion.

— Coordination is very important as in so many cases friendly troops unfortunately suffered casualties due to U.S. air strikes, artillery or utility tactical transport because of inadequate coordination. To minimize such accidents, the advisor should have sufficient information as to the tactical situation, especially, in a combined operation, where only the advisor can set up good coordination with the U.S. forces.

— Landing helicopter is usually limited, especially when a night defensive position is already set up. The counterpart realizes how anxious his advisor is to hear from home, however, he would appreciate it if the advisor would cancel his "mail drop" until the next morning in order to prevent the enemy from locating the battalion command post and shooting it up with his mortars sometime around midnight.

— After each operation the counterpart and his company commanders will get together and have a critique. It is a good occasion for the advisor to offer his comments. He should write them down if possible and give them to his counterpart prior to the meeting so that his counterpart has enough time to discuss them with him before adding to or improving his notes.

— The Vietnamese Marines will carry five days of rations consisting usually of: rice, dried and salted fishes or shrimps, canned sardines, soy sauce, and so forth. Of course the advisor is not required to eat Vietnamese ration if he does not want to; yet it is necessary for him to familiarize with and eat it if he wants the psychological advantage that he is sharing something with the host country.

— Eating Vietnamese food is sometimes difficult for western people. The typical meal for a middle class family consists usually of five types of food: one salted, one fried or roasted, a vegetable soup, some green vegetable and rice. "*Nuoc mam*," a fermented sauce made of fish and salt, is served in every meal and has a strong smell which is hard for westerners to taste. However, people of the North, Central and South have slightly different ways of preparing or serving their meal. Therefore, the type of meal that you will eat will depend on what part of the country your counterpart comes from. Try to eat all types of meals before judging the quality of Vietnamese food.

— Speaking fluent Vietnamese is not required of the advisor. The counterpart and most of his officers can understand English. Yet, if the advisor can realize how nice, friendly and sympathetic the Vietnamese people will feel when he can order foods in the host country's language or can use chop sticks skillfully, then he will try to learn something more than knowing the niceties of "good morning," "thank you" or "how are you."

— It is hard for westerners to learn Vietnamese because of its six tones, we might say a scale of six notes indicated by different symbols: the grave tone, the falling tone, the even tone, the interrogative tone, and the rising tone and the sharp tone. Each word, as it changes its tone, changes its meaning. Thus the word la changes it meaning accordingly as shown below: (*la*) to shout, (*la*) strange, (*la*) to be, (*la*) insipid, (*la*) lear.

— If we would say that advising is an art, then the smile would be an important factor which embellishes that art. A "sober face" and "know-it-all" will not get much chance to convince anyone. A Vietnamese saying goes "The smile costs no money to buy, but it buys many things."

— Usually, because of his prestige and self-respect, the counterpart is expected to solve his units' problems himself rather than seeking any advice. Therefore, understanding the counterpart, his problems and his unit is not a matter which can be achieved "from dawn to dusk," or possibly even in weeks, or months. The advisor must be patient and persistent and also a bit of a psychologist. An ancient Chinese proverb goes "if you know 'your enemy' and know yourself, you will win a hundred battles as you wish."

— There are many areas in which the advisor is not involved. One of these is the way your counterpart handles his internal problems, administratively and disciplinary, which are of course different than yours because of the influence of many factors, especially custom. The advisor must be realistic and understanding and try to keep his nose out of such cases.

— Remember that every 12 months, maybe less because of sickness or becoming a casualty, the counterpart gets a new advisor and each one has a different way of offering advice. Then the advisor leaves again, while his counterpart, still there, keeps confronting daily, many other problems and obstacles. The advisor must be delicate when offering advice and considerate when he feels his suggestions are not executed. Rather, the advisor should "advise slowly."

— Teamwork between the advisor, and his counterpart, and his staff officers will produce a harmonious and enthusiastic atmosphere. However, sometimes embarrassments cannot be avoided because of misunderstanding or the lack of coordination. For instance, information reported by an advisor through his advisory channel that is different from that of his counterpart to his task force commander, causing a feeling of distrust which hurts the teamwork spirit.

Conclusion

The advisor's mission and the part he must play are officially based on his professional knowledge and experiences. Of course, he must possess a great deal of knowledge concerning tactics and techniques, he must know the organization of his counterpart's unit as well as his host country's customs, history, language . . . Yet, he must know also the nature and character of the war that he is participating in as an advisor, the war whose from is not well-defined, the war where it is very difficult to recognize between friend and foe, the war that cannot be won by a military solution alone.

The Vietnamese Marines are proud to be known as South Vietnam's finest fighting force, and needless to say, they never deny the unselfish contributions of the U.S. Marine advisors coming from thousands of miles away and sharing their sacrifices. Of course, the assistance should not be superficial, but must be specified on a harmonious and sincere coordination, based on a solid friendship and relationship between two nations which are facing a common enemy: communism.

Techniques of Advising

Introduction

How does the advisor give advice? Each person must find the methods, which will produce results. Varying circumstances and personalities make it impossible to establish a rigid set of rules. This document has been prepared to give an insight into the complex job of Marine Advisor/diplomat. It represents the view, opinion, and recommendations of a number of experienced successful Marine Advisors. It is offered as guidance to new advisors.

It must be assumed that an officer assigned to the Marine Advisory Unit has broad experience and professional competence for this is the basic foundation for success. Upon reporting to the unit, the advisor should arm himself with as much information as possible concerning his duties. This can be accomplished by means of the "Job Description" provided by the Marine Advisory Unit, thorough briefing by the officer whom he is replacing--if possible, and a detailed study of all applicable directives concerned with duty in the Military Assistance Command, Vietnam.

Upon joining the Vietnamese Marine Battalion, the advisor should initially listen and observe closely. Until he begins to feel that he knows completely what is happening and why, suggestions should not be offered unless asked. He should remember that there have been many Americans before him, and his counterpart probably feels that he knows how to handle advisors. This will be the advisor's first--and probably last--experience of this nature; the Vietnamese experience this change constantly with the rotation of advisors.

General

The relationship between the advisor and counterpart must be based on the solid ground of competent professional knowledge, a mutual respect of services, and if possible, friendly personal contacts. The amalgamation of these will give best results. The advisor should at all times be himself, and not adopt a "new face" for dealings with his counterpart. The manner of extending advice or offering suggestions depends upon personalities, moods, and the situation. It has been found that using the same methods one would use to recommend a change of action to an American commander produces excellent results with the Vietnamese Commander. Quick changes are not to be expected and every effort should be made to continue the programs of the previous advisor, so that a continuity of programs and aims is apparent. The advisor should work from the "soft sell," with a gradual but persistent approach, featuring repetition of ideas and proposals. It is common, however, that the counterpart will not consider the new arrival as "his advisor" until the two have been exposed to combat together. The new advisor must have patience; the opportunity usually arrives in country.

"Rapport"

The word "rapport" which describes the harmony, accord, or affinity of the advisor with his counterpart is as nebulous to attain as it is to describe accurately. And it is perhaps an overworked word, since everyone seeks "rapport" without knowing what it is. To be sure, there must be developed between the advisor and his counterpart a workable, recognizable basis from which common goals can be achieved. Mutual respect between the two seems to be the first step. The advisor must learn all there is to know about his counterpart and the unit he commands, the problems of his command, and the strong points and weak points--both personal and professional--of the counterpart. To understand the commander will be to understand the command. Such knowledge will permit an honest interest in assisting the commander and his command without the inference of interference in the command.

The advisor must also earnestly strive to learn the customs, histories, taboos, superstitions of the Vietnamese people. He must learn to eat their food, and attend their social functions.

To know the commander/counterpart and to understand his problems, the advisor must be with the counterpart almost continually--without, however, "crowding" the counterpart. He likes his privacy as well as the fellow. But he must be made to know that the advisor will not participate in any personality clashes within the unit. The advisor's goal is to develop a genuine friendship and personal loyalty to his counterpart, which will not interfere with the advisor's professional relationship with his counterpart or objectivity to his job.

Assistance to the Unit

Since advisory duties involve all aspects of the battalion with which the advisor will work, the advisor will find that he must extend his influence through all levels of the command including the senior staff noncommissioned officers. It will often be necessary to give recommendations to, tutor, and encourage the staff officers as well as the company and platoon commanders. This must be done openly with no inference of usurping the Battalion Commander's authority. Generally, the commander will welcome such assistance.

The advisor must show interest in all facets of battalion operation and training, not solely the activities in which the Battalion Commander is directly concerned. The advisor must get out and look around, being alert to new practices or new procedures. He must talk to company commanders, platoon commanders, staff officers, and noncommissioned officer, learning their names and their interests. Only in this way will the advisor obtain a feel for the entire battalion. It will also help him know what is going on at all levels of command within the unit.

The advisor should take and interest in the dependents. Vietnamese are proud family men. They love their children, especially boys; and any genuine interest shown will have a great effect in cementing relationships. There is one caution in this respect. The advisor must not by word or expression express surprise or dismay at the primitive living and unsanitary conditions. Regardless of what the advisor may think, dependents are usually far better off than most civilians. Any improvements which the advisor can accomplish in this area should be low-keyed, except when the counterpart acknowledges unsatisfactory or below standard conditions.

As mentioned previously, in regards to social function, the advisor is expected to and should attend parties, ceremonies, and other functions to which he is invited. He should also be prepared to reciprocate social dinner engagements he may receive from the battalion officers. And he should make it a point to attend and participate wholeheartedly, in battalion athletic events.

The advisor, then, must spread his efforts far and wide to make his presence felt in the battalion. This is done with the primary purpose of assisting the battalion in every way possible, but not necessarily with the aim to display the American way of doing things.

Approaches, Attitudes, Techniques

There will be no attempt here to describe precisely how an advisor gives advice and counsel to his counterpart because this is influenced by many factors. The advisor will have to find this out for through cautions applications, with the hope that his intuition and innate good judgment will prevail. However, the following are considered basic methods of approach:

— Retain a sense of humor. There are many occasions during the advisor's tour where a sense of humor will be a necessity--and an advantage. The Vietnamese are happy people and like to laugh, sometimes in situations which might be considered under strange and morbid circumstances. It is not proposed that the advisor join a crowd in appreciation of the particular effect artillery has on the human body, reacting too quickly and violently to an incoming mortar round--and the Vietnamese will think that this is hilarious. At a time like this the only thing the advisor can do is laugh at himself with them.

— Always remember that the counterpart is the commanding officer. It is more practical for an advisor to proffer a suggestion prior to a commander's decision than it is to try to change a decision once it has been made. If there is any one point to be considered absolute doctrine, this is the one. And it behooves the advisor to be alert to anticipate decision through circumstances and make his suggestions accordingly. The commander can then gracefully accept the advice by appearing as though it was his idea in the first place.

— Do not outwardly display displeasure or disagreement with decisions, which have ignored the advice of the advisor. The advisor must make a decision on his own as to whether to fight for his principles, or to save his ammunition for another time, another place, a more important battle. Usually, the advisor finds it advantageous to wait. There have been many instances where the commander, realizing that the advice was good, has reversed himself on his own volition. Further, prodding by the advisor would have had the reverse effect of setting the commander's decision irrevocably. The advisor will find that demonstrations and examples will show the relative effectiveness of advisor ideas as compared with existing methods, and changes will eventually result.

— Never boast or attempt to take credit for practices or procedures which are implemented. The fact that the counterpart knows that the original idea was the advisor's is enough credit. This, too, is a vitally important point.

— Set a personal example of dress, bearing, industry, and initiative. The advisor must strive to be professionally correct and military in appearance at all times. The Vietnamese expect a U.S. Marine to be the epitome of strength, endurance, appearance, courage, and military skill. Though the advisor will seldom be aware of this, the Vietnamese will often compare their *Co-Van* with those of other Americans serving with the ARVN. The advisor must not let them down.

— Try to visit with U.S. Marine Units. The counterpart and his battalion are proud of the fact that they are Marines. When possible, the advisor should make and attempt to take his counterpart to visit a U.S. organization. With a little assistance and briefing by the advisor the USMC Commander can give the full "VIP" treatment to the counterpart, thus increasing his prestige. The visit also provides live training aids for programs in sanitation, staff functioning unit training, etc., which the advisor may be suggesting. The advisor will be surprised at the many practices which a Vietnamese battalion staff will adapt after they have watched a USMC battalion staff go through its paces.

— Understand the Vietnamese view. Usually, it is drastically different. But the advisor must realize that a valid suggestion cannot be accepted unless he understands the Vietnamese reason for doing something the way they have been doing it for years. The suggested changes have to be made with a view towards customs and circumstances.

— Give the counterpart time to think over a suggestion. The advisor must learn to offer new ideas or suggest new procedures sufficiently in advance of the need. He will sometimes find that a recommendation given yesterday is being put into practice tomorrow.

— Never lose your temper. This is a sign of weakness and must be avoided. It is permitted to be angry, but the advisor must retain control of his temper. This is not to suggest that occasionally a display of irritation is not appropriate. The advisor will often be irritated, but he must retain his composure most of the time. If a discussion becomes heated and the basic idea is being lost, the best idea is to forget it.

— Trivialities must not become unbearable. The advisor will find that many inconveniences are an inherent part of the advisor tasks; just grin and bear it.

— When deployed, a USMC advisor will spend about all of his time with the battalion. Advice offered during normal conversation, such as mealtime or during a break, allows the pros and cons of the suggestion to be discussed without the pressure of an immediate decision. The question and answer game also works. By asking questions, you can discover what the counterpart is thinking.

Remind him of items which may have forgotten. He can answer questions and give orders as though he were going to do it that way all along. And the job can be done before the break is over and the advisor can check.

— The advisor must be patient, persistent, and considerate. If the counterpart has demonstrated himself to be a competent leader, it then becomes the advisor's task to build the counterpart's confidence of his subordinates. By being selective in the problems to tackle, the advisor can help the counterpart achieve results which will encourage him to go on to bigger problems.

Approaches to Avoid

— Don't attempt the "hard sell" as a matter of habit. It may produce results occasionally, but as the counterpart becomes accustomed to this approach, it will be more difficult to employ. Be selective on the areas where the "hard sell" is to be used.

— Don't assume that some action will be accomplished as indicated in conversation with the counterpart. The advisor may be assured by his counterpart that orders have been issued. However, the advisor should follow up and do some discreet checking. Supervision will also be required.

— The Vietnamese have their internal and external politics, a different financial accounting system, and personal differences--many areas not involving the advisor. Advisors should keep abreast of such areas, but should not get involved except in matters which affect the battalion's ability to perform its basic functions.

— Don't attempt to win over the counterpart by ingratiating favors. When the advisor runs out of favors to do for the counterpart, he also runs out of influence.

— Don't be a combination supply officer and magician, pulling "goodies" from an inexhaustible supply hat. The advisor will invariably be asked to procure material for the counterpart through U.S. sources. This should be avoided by stubborn insistence that the Vietnamese supply system be made to work. Once the advisor embarks upon the role of supply officer, there will be no stop to it and he will end up merely an errand boy.

— Request will be received by advisors for purchases from the U.S. Exchange services. If the advisor honors one request, it will engender countless other requests. The best way out of the situation is to quote the exchange regulations. A bonafide gift under special circumstances may be warranted, but that should be the extent of the involvement.

— The "buddy system" or mutual admiration society in lieu of a sound professional basis and sincere personal respect is highly undesirable and offers no advantages.

— The Vietnamese system of officer-enlisted relationship and methods of inflicting commanding officer's punishment is very much different than what the advisor will be accustomed to. The advisor is cautioned not to intercede in any way. He should just try to understand the system--not change it.

Conclusion

The success of the advisor's efforts to win the respect and the cooperation of his Vietnamese counterpart is the direct equation of professional competence and knowledge multiplied by the amount of time that the advisor and counterpart spend together. In other words, the platform for a lasting and firm relationship is built slowly upon solid blocks of good advice. The officers of the Vietnamese Marine Corps are trained, experienced, and proud. The advisor, accordingly, should not expect his counterpart to come to him seeking advice. The advisor should be there, when he is needed, with an encouraging word, a possible recommendation, and enthusiastic support of the commander's eventual order. The patient but persistent advisor who hears his counterpart ask "What do you think?" has just been informed he is a success.

STANDING OPERATING PROCEDURES FOR MARINE ADVISORY UNIT

OFFICE OF THE SENIOR MARINE ADVISOR
Naval Advisory Group, Box #9
FPO San Francisco 96626

MAUO P5000.1A
0077: cjm

MARINE ADVISORY UNIT ORDER P5000.1A

From: Senior Marine Advisor
To: Distribution List

Subj: Standing Operation Procedures for Marine Advisory Unit

Encl: (1) Locator Sheet

    1. Purpose. To promulgate regulations, policies, responsibilities, restrictions and procedures for all personnel assigned to the Marine Advisory Unit.

    2. Cancellation. MAUO P5000.1.

    3. Effective Date. This order is effective upon promulgation.

    4. Certification. Revised and approved this date.

                                                                              J.W. Dorsey III

DISTRIBUTION: A

RECORD OF CHANGES

Log completed change action as indicated.				
Change Number	Date of Change	Date Received	Date Entered	Signature of person entering change

Table of Contents

Chapter I	Introduction and Responsibility	39
Chapter II	Mission, Billets and Billet Incumbent Tasks	43
Chapter III	Administration	61
Chapter IV	G-1 Advisory Element	73
Chapter V	G-2 Advisory Element [not in the original document]	85
Chapter VI	G-3 Advisory Element	87
Chapter VII	G-4 Advisory Element	91
Chapter VIII	Medical Administration	131
Chapter IX	Brigade Advisory Element	135
Chapter X	Artillery Advisory Element	139
Chapter XI	Field Deployment of Marine Advisory Unit	141
Chapter XII	Glossary of Terms and Abbreviations Used in RVN	169

MAUO P5000.1A
0077: cjm

Locator Sheet

Subj: Standing Operation Procedures for Marine Advisory Unit

See: _____
(Recipient enter information as to where this publication is maintained)

CHAPTER I
INTRODUCTION AND RESPONSIBILITY

PART I	**INTRODUCTION**	**PARAGRAPH**

SCOPE 1100

APPLICABILITY 1101

CHANGES 1102

PART II   RESPONSIBILITY

RESPONSIBILITY 1200

USE 1201

CHAPTER I
PART I: INTRODUCTION

1100 <u>SCOPE</u>

1. This order is a compilation of basic policies, regulation guidelines and procedures to be employed in the functioning of the Marine Advisory Unit; including those established by higher authority; and, where necessary, to clarify the intent of regulations as applicable to the Marine Advisory Unit.

1101 <u>APPLICABILITY</u>

1. This order shall be organized on a functional basis, utilization chapters as major divisions. The chapters are numbered in sequence and listed in the table of contents.

2. Paragraph numbering is based upon a four or five digit number which may be broken down as follows:

Example-1210.1a (1) (a): Chapter 1, Paragraph 210, Subparagraphs 1a, (1), (a)

1102 <u>CHANGES</u>

1. Changes to this order shall conform to established criteria and will be designed for insertion on a page for page basis.

2. A record of changes made will be maintained on the page provided for that purpose.

3. Holders are responsible for entering changes upon receipt.

CHAPTER I
PART II: RESPONSIBILITY

1200 <u>RESPONSIBILITY</u>

1. The current, accuracy and completeness of publication and distribution of this order and changes thereto are the responsibility of the Senior Marine Advisor. Normally, this responsibility shall be exercised through the Assistant Senior Marine Advisor and the Administrative Officer.

2. Cognizant Advisors are responsible for submitting recommended changes to the Senior Marine Advisor for publication and incorporation into this order.

1201 <u>USE</u>

1. This order is designed to assist all Advisors in day-to-day performance of duty.

2. This order will be used in conjunction with other regulations promulgated by the Senior Marine Advisor and higher authority.

3. Extra copies will be maintained by the Administrative Officer and will be included in the reading file for incoming advisors.

CHAPTER II
MISSION, BILLEST AND BILLET INCUMBENT TASKS

| PART I | MISSION | PARAGRAPH |

MISSION STATEMENT 2100

PART II BILLETS AND BILLET INCUMBENT TASKS

SENIOR MARINE ADVISOR 2200

ASSISTANT SENIOR MARINE ADVISOR 2201

ADMINISTRATIVE OFFICER 2202

G-1 ADVISOR 2203

PUBLIC AFFAIRS OFFICER
(Additional Duty of G-1 Advisor).........................2203.1

G-2/RECONNAISSANCE ADVISOR 2204

G-3 ADVISOR 2205

ASSISTANT G-3 ADVISOR 2205.1

OPERATIONS CHIEF 2205.2

POLWAR/PSYOPS OFFICER 2205.3
(Additional Duty of G-1 Advisor)

TRAINING ADVISOR 2205.4

TRAINING COMMAND ADVISOR 2205.5

G-4 ADVISOR 2206

SUPPLY ADVISOR 2206.1

COMMUNICATIONS ADVISOR 2206.2

ENGINEER ADVISOR 2206.3

43

ASSISTANT ENGINEER ADVISOR 2206.4

MOTOR TRANSPORT ADVISOR 2206.5

MOTOR TRANSPORT MECHANICAL ADVISOR 2206.6

ORDNANCE ADVISOR 2206.7

MEDICAL ADVISOR 2207

MEDICAL SERVICE ADVISOR 2207.1

BRIGADE ADVISOR 2208

ASSISTANT BRIGADE ADVISOR 2208.1

BRIGADE LIAISON OFFICER 2208.2

INFANTRY BATTALION ADVISOR 2208.3

ASSISTANT INFANTRY BATTALION ADVISOR 2208.4

DIVISION ARTILLERY ADVISOR 2209

ARTILLERY BATTALION ADVISOR 2209.1

ASSISTANT ARTILLERY BATTALION ADVISOR 2209.2

AMPHIBIOUS SUPPORT BATTALION ADVISOR 2210

CHAPTER II
PART I: MISSION

2100 <u>MISSION STATEMENT</u>

1. The mission of the Marine Advisory Unit is to establish a Vietnamese Marine Corps capable of conducting amphibious/riverine, airmobile and ground operations and to assist in establishing sound logistical and administrative procedures in order to enable the Vietnamese Marine Corps to conduct any assigned task benefit of U.S. Advisory Assistance.

2. A second and continuing mission is: to closely monitor the status of MASF supported equipment, and to inventory and inspect such equipment.

CHAPTER II
PART II: BILLETS AND BILLET INCUMBENT TASKS

2200 <u>SENIOR MARINE ADVISOR</u>

1. Tasks

    a. Confers as necessary with the Commandant and Chief of Vietnamese Marine Corps on advisory matters.

    b. Acts in a liaison capacity between the Chief, Naval Advisory Group and the Commandant, Vietnamese Marine Corps.

    c. Keeps the Chief, Naval Advisory Group fully informed on matters of interest occurring in the Marine Advisory Unit and in the Vietnamese Marine Corps.

    d. Directs the Marine Advisory Unit in the accomplishment of its assigned mission.

    e. Generates new initiatives which can be applied to problems of U.S. Marine Corps interest in the Vietnamese Marine Corps or within the Marine Advisory Unit.

    f. Coordinates, directs and guides the preparation of necessary studies, reports, and correspondence required by the Chief, Naval Advisory Group or higher authority.

    g. Makes recommendation to the Chief, Naval Advisory Group and Commandant, U.S. Marine Corps for changes in the organization and tasking of the Vietnamese Marine Corps and the Marine Advisory Unit.

    h. Is responsible to the Commandant, U.S. Marine Corps for administrative matters.

2201 <u>ASSISTANT SENIOR MARINE ADVISOR</u>

1. Tasks

    a. Directs, coordinates and supervises the activities of the Marine Advisory Unit Staff Advisors. Also, he assists the Senior Marine Advisor in the direction of field advisors.

    b. Is responsible for the routine administration of the Marine Advisory Unit.

    c. Promulgates approved plans, orders and instructions for the Marine Advisory Unit.

    d. Determines by personal observation, and with the assistance of Staff Advisors, the extent and effectiveness of execution of the Senior Marine Advisor's plans, orders, and instructions and recommends supplemental or corrective action when necessary.

e. Assembles, reviews and submits reports for the Senior Marine Advisor and directs distribution of approved reports.

f. Represents the Senior Marine Advisor when authorized and acts for the Senior Marine Advisor in his absence.

g. Confers on a frequent basis with the Chief of Staff, Vietnamese Marine Corps on advisory matters.

2202 ADMINISTRATIVE OFFICER

1. Tasks

a. Is responsible for planning and supervising matters and activities related to unit administration and internal operations of the Marine Advisory Unit Administrative Office.

b. Is responsible for processing official correspondence, preparation of records and reports, internal mail service, morale and special services activities, control of classified matter, preparation of recommendations for awards to U.S. personnel and casualty reporting.

c. Prepares directives for the enforcement of laws and regulation, troop conduct, appearance and administration of military justice.

d. Supervises the procurement, administration and control of civilian indigenous employees.

e. Performs other administrative matters not specifically assigned to another staff section.

f. Acts as the G-1 Advisor in the absence of the latter.

2203 G-1 ADVISOR

1. Tasks

a. Is responsible to the Assistant Chief of Staff, G-1, Vietnamese Marine Corps for providing professional advice in matters pertaining to personnel management and internal organization and operations of the Headquarters.

b. Assists the Assistant Chief of Staff, G-1, in specific areas of advisory effort which normally includes, but is not limited to, Personnel Statistics, Replacement and Desertion Control.

c. Coordinates all programs of a Civic Action or humanitarian nature and renders advice and assistance to all staff and field advisors in connection with those matters.

d. Acts as the Public Affairs Advisor to ensure timely publication of Civic Action efforts to all Vietnamese and Free World News Media, when appropriate.

e. Serves as the Administrative Officer in his absence.

f. Performs other administrative matters not specifically assigned to other staff sections.

g. Serves as an executive staff member to the Senior Marine Advisor and is responsible for TO&E changes, in coordination with the G-3 and G-4 Advisors, processing awards for Vietnamese Marine Corps personnel and the submission of timely changes to the JTD.

2203.1 PUBLIC AFFAIRS OFFICER (Additional Duty of G-1 Advisor)

1. Tasks

a. Acts as Advisor to the Public Affairs Officer of the Vietnamese Marine Corps by offering professional advice and guidance in information matters with the ultimate goal of a vigorous self-sufficient information office manned and operated by trained Vietnamese Marine Corps personnel and capable of enhancing the public image of the Vietnamese Marine Corps through the timely release of complete and factual information to the Free World news media in the form of written, recorded, and filmed news releases and general feature stories.

b. Maintains active liaison with Commander, U.S. Naval Forces, Vietnam, Public Affairs Officer, Military Assistance Command, Vietnam Office of Information, Advisory Division, Joint Public Affairs Office and members of the Free World Press, both military and civilian.

c. Acts as the English-speaking contact/liaison between the English-speaking free world press and the Vietnamese Marine Corps.

d. Acts as the Marine Advisory Unit Public Affairs Officer. To provide photographic coverage for release to military and hometown publications of decorations, promotions or other newsworthy events concerning Marine Advisory Unit personnel.

e. Collects, edits and publishes information of interest to and concerning the activities of Marine Advisory Unit personnel in a monthly publication, the CO-VAN.

2204 G-2/RECONNAISSANCE ADVISOR

1. Tasks

a. Advises the Assistant Chief of Staff, G-2, Vietnamese Marine Corps, on matters relative to the production of intelligence and use of intelligence and information.

b. Advises in matters pertaining to counterintelligence and the effort devoted to destroying the effectiveness of enemy or potential enemy intelligence activities.

c. Advises in and assists the Assistant Chief of Staff, G-2, Vietnamese Marine Corps, on matters pertaining to the intelligence input to plans and orders.

d. Advises and assists in the planning and supervising of intelligence training.

e. Advises and assists in the employment of ground reconnaissance units of the Vietnamese Marine Corps and coordination of reconnaissance and observation by infantry units, reconnaissance units and air observers.

f. Serves as an executive staff member to the Senior Marine Advisor.

2205 G-3 ADVISOR

1. Tasks

a. Is responsible for matters pertaining to organization, training and tactical operations.

b. Exercises staff responsible for advising and assisting the Assistant Chief of Staff, G-3, Vietnamese Marine Corps, in the areas of tactical operations, organization, equipment and training.

c. Directs, supervises and coordinates the efforts of the Assistant G-3 Advisor, Training Advisor, Training Command Advisor and Operations Chief.

d. Determines requirements for procurement and distribution of training aids, publications and facilities.

e. Prepares operational and historical reports.

f. Makes recommendations and does the planning for activation and/or deactivation of units of the Vietnamese Marine Corps.

g. In conjunction with the G-4 Advisor, recommends additions and/or deletions in Military Assistance Service Funded material in the Vietnamese Marine Corps Tables of Organization and Equipment.

h. Serves as an executive staff member to the Senior Marine Advisor.

2205.1 ASSISTANT G-3 ADVISOR

1. Tasks

a. Performs assigned duties under the cognizance of the G-3 Advisor.

b. Is responsible for the routine administration of the G-3 Advisory element to include:

(1) Preparation of the weekly Summary of Vietnamese Marine Corps Operations and Advisory Efforts.

(2) Preparation of the monthly Historical Summary.

(3) Any other assigned tasks.

2205.2 OPERATIONS CHIEF

1. Tasks

    a. Performs assigned duties under the cognizance of the G-3 Advisor.

    b. Is responsible for the following tasks:

       (1) Daily contact with Vietnamese Marine Corps combat operations center.

       (2) Update operational map daily.

       (3) Brief Senior Marine Advisor daily on Vietnamese Marine Corps operations.

       (4) Preparation of daily Situation Report and NOC unit Location Report.

       (5) Twice daily radio communication with operational units.

       (6) Assist G-3 Advisor with weekly and monthly reports.

       (7) Perform any other assigned tasks.

2205.3 POLWAR/PSYOPS OFFICER (Additional Duty of G-1 Advisor)

1. Tasks

    a. Performs assigned duties under the cognizance of the Senior Marine Advisor.

    b. Is responsible for all political warfare and psychological operations efforts of the unit.

    c. Conducts such liaison as may be required with higher headquarters to enhance his efforts and knowledge and that of his counterpart.

    d. Completes reports as required by senior headquarters in connection with Psychological Operations and Political Warfare efforts.

    e. Assists his counterpart in submitting reports as required through Vietnamese channels.

f. Acts as a special staff officer to the Senior Marine Advisor.

   g. Acts as the Marine Advisory Unit Civic Actions Officer.

2205.4 TRAINING ADVISOR

1. Tasks

   a. Performs assigned duties under the cognizance of the G-3 Advisor.

   b. Provides advice to the Training Officer, Vietnamese Marine Corps, in those areas pertaining to military training management.

   c. Monitors that portion of the Military Assistance Service Funded Offshore Training Program supporting the Vietnamese Marine Corps.

   d. Monitors that portion of the RVNAF supported In-Country Training Program supporting the Vietnamese Marie Corps.

   e. Serves as a special staff officer to the Senior Marine Advisor.

2205.5 TRAINING COMMAND ADVISOR

1. Tasks

   a. Performs assigned duties under the cognizance of the G-3 Advisor.

   b. Provides advice to the Commanding Officer, Training Command, Vietnamese Marine Corps in those areas pertaining to military training management.

   c. Exercise supervisory control of the Assistant Training Command Advisor.

2206 G-4 ADVISOR

1. Tasks

   a. Is responsible for matters pertaining to supply, transportation, communications and engineer and maintenance assistance.

   b. Exercises staff responsibility for advising the Assistant Chief of Staff, G-4, Vietnamese Marine Corps in matters pertaining to supply, evacuation and hospitalization, service and miscellaneous related subjects.

   c. Directs, supervises and coordinates the efforts of Supply, Communications, Engineer, Motor Transport and Ordnance Advisors.

d. Is responsible for the Military Assistance Service Funded (MASF) Program for the Vietnamese Marine Corps. This responsibility includes determination of requirements, introduction of new items, and determination of the replenishment factor for material in use or on order.

e. Prepares the semiannual (15 Apr - 15 Oct) validation of End Use of MASF equipment when required.

f. Is responsible for the coordination of the annual MASF inventory.

g. Serves as an executive staff member to the Senior Marine Advisor.

2206.1 SUPPLY ADVISOR

1. Tasks

a. Under the cognizance of the G-4 Advisor, the Supply Advisor provides advisory assistance to the Supply officer, Vietnamese Marine Corps.

b. Plans, coordinates and supervises all supply functions for the Marine Advisory Unit.

c. Assists the G-4 Advisor in the monitoring of the MASF program.

d. Maintains an inventory, requisition and status card on each item of MASF equipment.

e. Assists in the conduct of the annual MASF inventory.

2206.2 COMMUNICATIONS ADVISOR

1. Tasks

a. Under the cognizance of the G-4 Advisor, the Communications Advisor provides advice and assistance in planning employment and maintenance of communications to the Vietnamese Marine Corps Communications-Electronics Officer as well as the Commanding Officer, Communications Company, Headquarters Battalion, and communications officers of the separate battalions of the Vietnamese Marine Corps.

b. Acts as the staff communications officer of the Marine Advisory Unit, providing technical assistance, equipment and maintenance support to the U.S. Marine Corps Advisors.

c. Coordinates communications matters of the Marine Advisory Unit with the Communications Officer, U.S. Naval Forces, Vietnam.

2206.3 ENGINEER ADVISOR

1. Tasks

   a. Is responsible to the G-4 Advisor for providing professional advice to the Vietnamese Marine Corps in all aspects of military engineering, including combat engineer support; planning and construction; and maintenance of all facilities.

   b. Advises the Commanding Officer, Engineer Battalion and the Assistant Chief of Staff, G-4, Vietnamese Marine Corps on all engineering and facilities maintenance matters. Provide technical assistance to the Amphibious Support Battalion Advisor for Shore Party matters.

   c. Serves as a special staff advisor to the Marine Advisory Unit.

   d. Maintains a map supply for the Marine Advisory Unit.

   e. Plans, programs and supervises the execution of the Military Assistance Construction Program and the Joint Service Construction Program.

   f. Assists the Vietnamese Marine Corps in planning and programming requirements for dependents housing.

2206.4 ASSISTANT ENGINEER ADVISOR
1. Tasks

   a. Performs assigned duties under the cognizance of the Engineer Advisor.

   b. Coordinates the self-help constructing program to include material acquisition and delivery.

   c. Advises the Commanding Officer, Engineer Construction Company on all aspects of military construction.

   d. Advises the Base Camp Commanders on matters relating to facilities maintenance and operation of utilities.

2206.5 MOTOR TRANSPORT ADVISOR

1. Tasks

   a. Under the staff cognizance of the G-4 Advisor the Motor Transport Advisor provides advisory assistance to the Vietnamese Marine Corps on all aspects of transportation with emphasis on motor transport operations and maintenance.
   b. Advises the Vietnamese Marine Corps Transportation Officer and the Commanding Officer, Transportation Company on the following:

   (1) Maintaining records and submitting reports.

(2) Supervising the determination of requirements for requisitioning, receipt, storage, distribution and documentation of motor transport vehicles, equipment, and supplies.

(3) Monitoring repair parts requirements and ensuring that units of the Vietnamese Marine Corps have authorized levels on hand as prescribed by Parts Load Lists and appropriate technical manuals.

(4) Conducting technical inspections of motor equipment.

(5) Inspecting motor transport personnel and unit vehicle and maintenance records.

(6) Maintaining technical motor transport training programs and ensuring its adequacy to support Vietnamese Marine Corps requirements.

(7) Preparing plans and recommendations for availability and employment of transportation resources organic to and supporting the Vietnamese Marine Corps.

(8) Monitoring equipment maintenance and repair being performed by units and activities supporting the Vietnamese Marine Corps.

c. Serves as a special staff officer to the Senior Marine Advisor for matters pertaining to motor transport. These duties include:

(1) Functioning as Advisor Vehicle Coordinator for the purpose of coordinating the authorization level, distribution, operation, maintenance, and security of advisor vehicles.

(2) Acting as licensing officer for the Marine Advisory Unit for issuing U.S. Government Motor Vehicle Operator's Permits and obtaining Vietnamese Driver's License.

(3) Conducting an annual inventory of all Motor Transport Military Assistance Service Funded (MASF) items.

2206.6 MOTOR TRANSPORT MECHANICAL ADVISOR

1. Tasks

a. Performs assigned duties under the immediate supervision and cognizance of the Motor Transport Advisor.
b. Provides detailed advice and recommendations to Motor Transport Maintenance personnel at the unit level in the following areas:
(1) Organization of unit maintenance facilities.

(2) Proper maintenance and repair procedures on unit motor transport equipment.

(3) Correct use of tool and test sets and chests, and technical publications an manuals.

(4) Proper procedures for requisitioning and storing spare/repair parts.

2206.7 ORDNANCE ADVISOR

1. Tasks

a. Under the cognizance of the G-4 Advisor, the Ordnance Advisor provides technical advisory assistance to the Assistant Chief of Staff, G-4, VNMC and his designated Division Ordnance Officer on ordnance matters.

b. Supervises the determination of requirements for, and the requisitioning, procurement, storage, and distribution of ordnance materiel, i.e., weapons, optical, ammunition, etc.

c. Makes estimates of operational ammunition requirements, establishing priorities, and monitoring mount out ammunition allowances and the issuing of ammunition for training and combat within established priorities and allowances.

d. Plans and supervises the recovery, evacuation, and maintenance of ordnance material beyond the capability of using units.

e. Coordinates the establishment and operation of ordnance maintenance and supply activities.

f. Provides for technical inspection of ordnance material, including organizational maintenance of such material.

h. Plans and supervises explosive ordnance disposal.

2207   MEDICAL ADVISOR

1. Tasks

a. Is responsible for providing assistance and advice to the Vietnamese Marine Corps' Division Surgeon and Commanding Officer, Medical Battalion, in the areas of medical supply, training, preventive medicine, hygiene, sanitation, and safety as well as the medical aspects of psychological warfare.

b. Directs, supervises and coordinates the efforts of the Assistant Medical Advisor.

c. Serves as a special staff advisor to the Marine Advisory Unit.

2207.1 MEDICAL SERVICE ADVISOR

1. Tasks

a. Assists the Medical Advisor in the various areas of medical advisory interest.

b. Performs routine sick call for members of the Marine Advisory Unit.

c. Assumes duties of the Medical Advisor during the absence of the latter.

2208 BRIGADE ADVISOR

1. Tasks

a. Advises the Vietnamese Marine Corps Brigade Commander on matters relative to organization, employment, tactics and logistical support and utilization of supporting arms of the Brigade combat and combat support elements.

b. Advises and assists the Brigade staff in the planning of operations and in correct staff functioning.

c. Is responsible for the establishment of liaison with Free World Forces in combined operation, liaison and coordination with Free World Forces in supporting roles, liaison with Free World Advisors assigned to other Republic of Vietnam Armed Forces and for scheduling, coordinating and employing of Free World provided supporting arms.

d. Is responsible for the continued effective execution of the directives, policies and instructions of the Senior Marine Advisor pertaining to the Marine Advisory Unit as well as policies and directives of higher headquarters.

e. Coordinates the activities of all other Marine field advisors which are operating in the same geographical area.

2208.1 ASSISTANT BRIGADE ADVISOR

1. Tasks

a. Serves as principle assistant to the Brigade Advisor and acts as the coordinator of supporting arms for the Brigade.
b. Acts for the Brigade Advisor in his absence.

c. Performs such other duties as may be assigned by the Brigade Advisor.

2208.2 BRIGADE LIAISON OFFICER

1. Tasks

a. Is responsible to the Senior Brigade Advisor in the performance of his duties.

b. Depending upon the tactical field location of the Brigade, he may be located with the Senior Brigade Advisor at the Command Post, or at times, separated, depending upon the proximity of the Command Post to the OPCON Headquarters.

    c. Monitors/coordinates Brigade logistics effort when U.S. assets are employed.

    d. Coordinates logistical support between the Marine Advisory Unit and field advisors.

    e. Monitors Vietnamese Marine Corps medical evacuation procedures if medical facilities are located in the immediate area, as when U.S. dust offs are utilized.

2208.3 INFANTRY BATTALION ADVISOR

1. Tasks

    a. Advises the Vietnamese Marine Corps Infantry Battalion Commander of matters relative to organization, employment, tactics and logistical support of the battalion.

    b. Advises, instructs and influences the battalion staff in the planning of operations and in correct staff functions.

    c. In the absence of the Brigade Advisor, he is responsible for the establishment of liaison with Free World Forces in join operations, liaison and coordination with Free World Forces in supporting roles, liaison with Free World Advisors with Republic of Vietnam Forces and for scheduling, coordinating and employment of Free World provided supporting arms.

    d. Is responsible for the continued effective execution of the directives, policies and instructions of the Senior Marine Advisor pertaining to the Marine Advisor Unit.

    e. Monitors the Military Assistance Program within the battalion.

    f. Coordinates the activities of the Assistant Infantry Battalion Advisor.

2208.4 ASSISTANT INFANTRY BATTALION ADVISOR

1. Tasks

    a. Serves as the principle assistant to the Infantry Battalion Advisor and acts as the coordinator of supporting arms for the battalion.

    b. Acts for the Infantry Battalion Advisor in his absence.

    c. Performs such other duties as may be assigned by the Brigade or Infantry Battalion Advisors.

2209   DIVISION ARTILLERY ADVISOR

1. Tasks

    a. Advises the Vietnamese Marine Corps Division Artillery Commander on matters relative to organization, employment, tactical fire direction, fire support coordination and logistical support of the division artillery.

    b. Advises, instructs and influences the division artillery staff in the planning of operations and in correct staff functioning.

    c. Is responsible for the establishment of liaison with Free World Forces in joint operations, liaison and coordination with Free World Forces in supporting roles, liaison with Free World Advisors assigned to other Republic of Vietnam Armed Forces and for scheduling, coordinating and employing of Free World provided supporting arms.

    d. Is responsible for the continued effective execution of the directives, policies and instructions of the Senior Marine Advisor pertaining to the Marine Advisory Unit, as well as policies and directives of higher headquarters.

    e. Coordinates the activities of the Artillery Battalion Advisors.

2209.1 <u>ARTILLERY BATTALION ADVISOR</u>

1. Tasks

    a. Advises the Vietnamese Marine Corps' Artillery Battalion Commander on matters relative to organization, employment, tactical fire direction, fire support coordination and logistic support of the battalion.

    b. Advises, instructs and influences the battalion staff in the planning of operations and in correct staff functioning.

    c. Is responsible for the establishment of liaison with Free World Forces in joint operations, liaison and coordination with Free World Forces in supporting roles, liaison with Free World Advisors with other Republic of Vietnam Armed Forces and for scheduling, coordinating and employing of Free World provided supporting arms.

    d. Monitors the Military Assistance Service Funded program in the battalion.

    e. Coordinates the activities of the Assistant Artillery Battalion Advisor.

    f. Acts for the Division Artillery Advisor when designated.

    g. Performs such other duties as may be assigned by the Division Artillery Advisor.

2209.2 <u>ASSISTANT ARTILLERY BATTALION ADVISOR</u>

1. Tasks

   a. Serves as the principle assistant to the Artillery Battalion Advisor.

   b. Acts for the Artillery Battalion Advisor when designated.

   c. Performs such other duties as may be assigned by the Artillery Battalion Advisor.

2210   AMPHIBIOUS SUPPORT BATTALION ADVISOR

1. Tasks

   a. Is responsible for the establishment of liaison with Free World Forces in joint operations, liaison and coordination with Free World Forces in supporting roles, liaison with Free World Advisors with other Republic of Vietnam Armed Forces and for scheduling, coordinating and employing of Free World provided supporting arms.

   b. Advises and assists the battalion staff in correct staff functioning.

   c. Is responsible for the establishment and liaison with Free World Forces in combined operations.

   d. Assists in establishing effective logistical support for operating units by liaison and coordination with the Republic of Vietnam Armed Forces.

   e. Is responsible for the continued effective execution of the directives, policies and instructions of the Senior Marine Advisor pertaining to the Marine Advisory Unit as well as policies and directives of higher headquarters.

   f. Monitors the Military Assistance Program within the battalion.

   g. Assists the Marine Advisory Unit G-4 Advisor in coordinating the activities of the special staff advisor within his cognizance.

CHAPTER III
ADMINISTRATION

| PART II | PERSONNEL MATTERS | PARAGRAPH |

PROCESSING NEW ARRIVALS 3100

BILLETING 3101

CURRENCY CONTROL 3102

MESSING FACILITIES 3103

DAILY ROUTINE 3104

EMERGENCY NOTIFICATION PLAN 3105

ABSENCE BY REASON OF ILLNESS OR INJURY 3106

DISBURSING 3107

CHECK-OUT POINTS 3108

PART II   FITNESS REPORTS

FITNESS REPORTS 3200

PART III   SECURITY OF CLASSIFIED MATTER

BACKGROUNDS 3300

AUTHORITY TO CLASSIFY CORRESPONDENCE 3301

PREPARATION AND MARKING 3302

CUSTODY AND ACCOUNTING 3303

SAFE COMBINATIONS 3304

DESTRUCTION PROCEDURES 3305

SECURITY VIOLATIONS AND COMPRISE 3306

CHAPTER III
PART I: PERSONNEL MATTERS

3100   PROCESSING NEW ARRIVALS

1. Upon notification of assignment of personnel to the Marine Advisory Unit, the Administration Officer will prepare and forward a welcome aboard letter to the incoming advisor. A recommended minimum uniform and civilian clothing list, job description and a copy of the Vietnamese Marine Corps rank structure will be enclosed with the welcome aboard letter.

    a. Upon receipt of information of the departure date from CONUS flight number of incoming personnel, the Administrative Officer will verify the time and date of arrival in Vietnam of the incoming flight. Every effort will be made to meet new personnel at Tan Son Nhut Air Base and assist in any way possible. The Assistant Senior Marine Advisor will make every effort to also greet incoming advisors.

3101   BILLETING

1. Personnel of the Marine Advisory Unit are billeted in either the Splendid BOQ or Plaza BEQ. The rooms are assigned on a space available basis and may require the acceptance of temporary billeting in another facility until a vacancy occurs. Minimum charge for room (maid) service is 975 piasters monthly for enlisted and 1,025 piasters monthly for officers. A minimum charge for laundry service is an additional 1,475 piasters monthly.

3102   CURRENCY CONTROL

1. Currency for internal transactions within military facilities and in use by the United States is Military Payment Certificate (MPC). Upon arrival in Vietnam personnel must convert United States currency (green) to MPC. This should be accomplished at the Tan Son Nhut Air Base terminal upon arrival in country.

2. The following is the approved rate of exchange of MPC for piasters:

                MPC $1.00 = 410 piasters

3. Military Payment Certificates can be converted to piasters at many of the military facilities and banks in the Saigon/Cholon area. Converting any currency at an unauthorized outlet is illegal.

3103   MESSING FACILITIES

1. U.S. Army Field Ration Mess facilities are available in many BOQs/BEQs within the immediate area. Meals are sold at the field ration messes to personnel on commuted rations. The charges are as follows:

	Enlisted Officer Food Cost	Officer Food Cost	Total Surcharge	Charges
Breakfast	$ .25	$ .25	$ .10	$ .35
Lunch	.55	.50	.10	.60
Dinner	.70	.65	.15	.80

3104 **DAILY ROUTINE**

1. Normal working hours for military personnel of the Marine Advisory Unit are from 0730 to 1800, Monday through Friday and 0730 to 1200 on Saturday. Normal working hours for civilian personnel of the Marine Advisory Unit are from 0730 to 1730, Monday through Friday and 0730 to 1200 on Saturday.

2. Staff Advisors will check out with their section head or the Assistant Senior Marine Advisor when departing the unit for extended periods during normal working hours.

3105 **EMERGENCY NOTIFICATION PLAN**

1. Certain plans and instructions received from higher echelons of command may require immediate notification of personnel attached to the Marine Advisory Unit. The Duty Officer will contact the following personnel in the order listed, in the event of implementation of contingency or other instructions requiring immediate action during other than normal working hours:

Assistant Senior Marine Advisor
Senior Marine Advisor

2. Names of all Marine Advisory Unit personnel are contained in a unit billeting roster on the Administrative Officer's desk indicating quarters' assignment and quarters' phone number. All advisors are to ensure their names and phone numbers are contained on the billeting roster with current information.

3106 **ABSENCE BY REASON OF ILLNESS OR INJURY**

1. Marine Advisory Unit personnel who are incapable of performing their duties because of illness or injury will immediately inform the Administrative Officer of their absence and prognosis.

3107 **DISBURSING**

1. The disbursing office servicing the Marine Advisory Unit is located in the MACV Annex. The disbursing office handles all pay matters including regular pay, travel pay, dependent's travel and dislocation allowance. Because of the volume of travel claims to be processed, travel claims normally will require approximately ten days for liquidation upon arrival in country.

a. Pay procedures. Pay and allowances are computed to the 15th and 30th day of each month. Pay is by Military Payment Certificate check and pay days are normally on the 15th and last day of each month.

(1) A representative of the administrative office will pick up the pay checks on each payday and either deliver them to the individual or deposit them into established bank account. To have the check deposited automatically on each payday, the administrative office will be furnished with an appropriate number of deposit slips for the checking account. Personnel will be furnished with an appropriate number of deposit slips for the checking slip receipts as soon as possible after the checks have been deposited, and the original deposit slip filed in a personal file, available upon request.

b. Checking Accounts. Checking accounts may be established at either the Bank of America, the Chase Manhattan Bank or the American International Banking Corporation who are all authorized to operate Military Banking Facilities in RVN. All offer the same services of a free checking account plus 5% per annum interest, computed monthly for maintaining a minimum balance of at least $100.00 for a full calendar month. Details are covered in Military Assistance Command, Vietnam Directive 37-30 which is available from the Administrative Officer.

c. Saving Deposits Program. Personnel may deposit any amount of five dollars or more, in multiples of five dollars, which is not in excess of their current unallotted pay and allowances, into the Savings Deposit Program. Deposits may be by cash or allotment deduction. Interest will accrue on amounts deposited at the annual rate of 10% (compounded quarterly). A withdrawal can be made only in an emergency when the health or welfare of the member or his dependents would be jeopardized if the withdrawal was not granted. The allotment for saving deposits can be stopped upon the request of the member or upon the member's return to the United States.

3108 CHECK-OUT POINTS

1. The rotation date for members of the Marine Advisory Unit is established as the day prior to the date the individual departed from CONUS, and is referred to locally as the DEROS (Date Eligible to Return from Oversees). Personnel may be booked up to seven days prior to DEROS. Exceptions will be made for personnel with release dates which require booking outside this time frame to ensure arrival at the new duty station by a specific date. The Senior Marine Advisor's policy is to release personnel at least two days prior to their DEROS. A release date will be assigned in accordance with the following:

a. Member is in a key position and retention to a particular date is necessary to provide required overlap with replacement.

b. Member has been given a directed reporting or detachment date in PCS orders.

    c. Member's relief reported early, complete turnover has been made, and operational commitments would not be curtailed by this early departure.

    d. As directed by the Senior Marine Advisor.

2. The Administrative Officer will commence checking out outgoing personnel at approximately 60 days prior to their DEROS utilizing the Check-Off List contained in TAB A. The second page of the Check-Off List contains pertinent information for personnel departing Vietnam. This form is given to personnel to use as a guide while checking out.

CHAPTER III
PART II: FITNESS REPORTS

3200 FITNESS REPORTS (Revised-see Marine Advisory Unit Order 1610.1)

CHAPTER III
PART III: SECURITY OF CLASSIFIED MATTER

3300   BACKGROUNDS

1. The Security Manual for Classified Matter (OPNAVINST 5510.1C) contains detailed regulations and guidance for classifying, marking and handling of classified matter, and for access thereto and disclosure. COMNAVFORV/CHNAVADVGRP Staff Organization and Regulations Manual, Chapter 16 (NAVFORV/NAVADVGR INST 5400.1A) contains additional local requirements and guidance relative to classified material. The foregoing directive shall be adhered to by the Marine Advisory Unit.

3301   AUTHORITY TO CLASSIFY CORRESPONDENCE

1. Top secret classification authority is held by COMNAVFORV. Secret and Confidential classification authority is hereby delegated to Marine Advisory Unit personnel authorized to sign correspondence by direction.

3302   PREPARATION AND MARKING

1. Procedures will be established to ensure proper control and supervision of classified correspondence preparation and marking. Particular attention will be given to Vietnamese security classifications and special handling markings for foreign dissemination or releasing.

   a. Classified Material Control Officer. The Administrative Officer is the Classified Material Control Officer. Other administrative personnel may be designated to perform administrative matters in support of the Classified Material Control Officer.

3303   CUSTODY AND ACCOUNTING

1. The Classified Material Control Officer will establish procedures to ensure accountability and custody of all classified material under his cognizance.

   a. Individual Responsibility. Security of classified material is the responsibility of the user, i.e., anyone in possession or having knowledge of classified material. In Vietnam, this responsibility assumes increased importance. From preparation to handling, stowage, accountability and final disposition, all users must exercise the utmost care to ensure that classified matter does not become available to unauthorized personnel. Careless disclosure of classified and sensitive information by personnel will have an adverse affect on the capability of the Marine Advisory Unit to perform its mission. Personnel are cautioned to double efforts to ensure that information of this type is not disclosed to personnel who do not have a "need to know." Specifically, advisors must carefully consider matter to be discussed over the telephone. In addition, care must be taken when discussing information with personnel who have a "need to know," that other personnel in the vicinity are not within hearing range who do not have a bona fide requirement for the data.

(1) Care must be taken in the handling of notes, classified documents and other sensitive material to ensure that these matters do not fall into the hands of those who do not have a legitimate requirement. Classified or sensitive material must be retained in the individual's possession when not secured in accordance with pertinent security regulation. This information must not be placed on even a temporary basis where access may be obtained by unauthorized personnel. Personnel are cautioned not to maintain classified and sensitive matter in their quarters. Classified and sensitive matter, not maintained in the Marine Advisory Unit's S&C Vault, should be in the personal possession of an individual having a requirement for its use or should be locked in a suitable container, inaccessible to others without a "need to know." All secret material taken from the Marine Advisory Unit S&C Vault will be receipted for by use of the check out log provided.

3304 SAFE COMBINATION

1. The Classified Material Control Officer shall maintain the vault for storage of all classified material within the Marine Advisory unit. Combinations to the vault and safe will be placed in combination change envelopes and delivered to the Classified Material Control Officer, Headquarters, U.S. Naval Forces, Vietnam.

3305 DESTRUCTION PROCEDURES

1. In an emergency involving the danger of capture of classified matter, the importance of beginning its destruction sufficiently early cannot be overemphasized. The consequences of such destruction, which may be determined as a matter of hindsight to have been unnecessary, may be relatively unimportant when measured against the possibility of compromise through capture. When possible, the Classified Material Control Officer or his alternate will have the direct control of and responsibility for the implementation of the destructive plan.

a. Although the Classified Material Control Officer is directly responsible for emergency destruction, the exercise by all personnel of the highest degree of individual initiative practicable to accomplish the destruction of classified documents and material is expected. In extreme situations destruction will be carried out by any means possible.

b. Emergency destruction instructions will be posted in the immediate vicinity of all classified document containers. Additionally, priority of destruction sheets will be affixed to each container. Burn priority will be indicated on the front of each drawer of the safe and filing cabinets.

c. Safes and filing cabinets containing classified and unclassified material are located inside the vault in the Administrative Officer's office and in the offices of the G-1, G-3 and G-4 Advisors. The combinations to the vault and Safe #1 inside the vault may be obtained from the Classified Material Control Officer, Office of the Administrative Assistant to the Chief of Staff, NAVFORV (Code 021), located on the second deck, Headquarters, U.S.

Naval Forces, Vietnam. Telephone 922-4663. In the event of an emergency, vault and safe combinations can be obtained via telephone.

    d. In the event of an emergency requiring removal or destruction of classified matter, the emergency destruction plan posted on the door of the vault should be carried out by any person present.

    (1) Destruction reports shall be filled out on all classified material in the normal manner, provided there is sufficient time to accomplish this action.

    (2) Priority of destruction shall be in the order listed in the destruction plan. This unit does not hold Top Secret documents.

    (3) The Vietnamese security classification of MAT and KIN will be destroyed in order prescribed for SECRET and CONFIDENTIAL documents, respectively.

    (4) Logs/registers are to be saved for accounting purposes.

    e. In the event of imminent capture or compromise of classified material through an enemy attack, burn all material IMMEDIATELY, i.e., removal from the container and burning on the floor, in the priority of destruction listed in the destruction plan. An incineration device is located on top of the storage containers for this purpose. Logs/registers are to be saved, if possible for accounting purposes.

3306   <u>SECURITY VIOLATIONS AND COMPROMISES</u>

1. Any person in the Marine Advisory Unit receives information that classified material or information has been lost, compromised or subjected to compromise, shall report the facts immediately to the Classified Material Control Officer.

TAB A--CHECK OFF LIST (Commence two months in advance of DEROS)

_____

NAME,   RANK,   SER. NO   DEROS

1. Submit recommendation for RNV award to AC/S, AG, VNMC: _____

2. Request War Trophy Souvenir Weapon: _____

3. Provide change of address cards to advisor to stop in-coming mail, e.g., magazines, newspapers, etc. prior to DEROS: _____

4. Obtain recommended fitness report markings for any subordinate advisors: _____

CHECK-OFF LIST (Commence when required)

5. Orders received from CMC?   _____

6. Orders received on relief? _____ due in: _____

7. Date to be returned from field for check out: _____

8. Plaque ordered: _____

9. Date of RVN awards presentation: _____

10. Flight request received and returned to MCPS: _____

11. Departure flight info: Date: _____ Check-in: _____ Depart: _____

12. Final fitness report submitted to SMA: _____

13. Recommended rough fitness report markings submitted to SMA: _____

14. Special Service gear turned in: _____

15. Recommended meritorious service award submitted.   _____

16. Urinalysis test (MCPS 96-72 hours prior to DEROS):   _____

17. Pick up orders from MCPS (If original orders are picked up within 24 24 hours of departure, disbursing will pay advance travel in U.S. dollars):   _____

18. Ship Household/Personal effects (Advance copies of orders are provided

to accomplish this up to 30 days prior to DEROS: _____

19. Register War Trophy Souvenir Weapon (Take weapon to N2 NAVFORV for registration certificate, them to the PMO at 19 Gia Long for customs clearance forms: _____

20. Turn 782 gear and weapon into MACV Supply Section: _____

21. Pick up Pay Record at disbursing: _____

22. Turn communications gear in to Communications Advisor: _____

23. Ensure that you have the following items in your possession upon departure:

Orders _____
OQR/SRB _____
Health and Dental Records _____
Pay Record _____
Shot Card (Up-to-date) _____

24. Have an eight-week supply of antimalaria pills with you: _____

25. Transfer/close bank account: _____

26. Check out of BOQ/BEQ: _____

27. Arrange transportation to airport: _____

CHAPTER IV
G-1 ADVISORY ELEMENT

| PART I | G-1 PERSONNEL MATTERS | PARAGRAPH |

ORGANIZATION 4100

BRIEFING OF NEW ARRIVALS 4101

REPORTS AND REPORTING 4102

PART II AWARDS PROGRAM

SUBMISSION OF AWARD RECOMMENDATIONS 4200

APPROVAL OF AWARDS 4201

PRESENTATION OF AWARDS 4202

PART III PUBLIC AFFAIRS ADVISOR

PUBLIC AFFAIRS OFFICER (PAO) BRIEFING .4300

BIOGRAPHICAL FILES 4301

PHOTOGRAPHY 4302

PRESS PHOTOGRAPHY 4303

FILM SUPPLY 4304

NEWS MEDIA RELATIONSHIPS 4305

MONTHLY NEWSLETTER 4306

CHAPTER IV
PART I: G-1 PERSONNEL MATTERS

4100 <u>ORGANIZATION</u>

1. The G-1 Advisory Element is composed of the G-1 Advisor and Public Affairs Advisor and is responsible only to the Assistant Senior Marine Advisor. All administrative support is provided by the Administrative Section of the Marine Advisory Unit.

4101 <u>BRIEFING OF NEW ARRIVALS</u>

1. The G-1 Advisor briefs each incoming advisor on personnel procedures within the Vietnamese Marine Corps. The briefing includes the following personnel areas and also associated day-to-day happenings.

    a. Authorized strength vs Assigned strength

    b. Promotions

    c. Rank and MOS assignments

    d. Testing and classification

    e. Pay and allowances

    f. Vietnamese Marine Corps housing and other benefits

    g. Recruiting

    h. Desertion and disciplinary procedures

    i. Vietnamese Marine Corps awards program

    j. Civic Action Programs

    k. Leave and liberty

    l. Biographic Reporting (Classified)

    m. Vietnamese Marine Corps Information Section

4102 REPORTS AND REPORTING PROCEDURES

1. The G-1 Advisor provides input to the Senior Marine Advisor, other Advisors and certain Military Assistance Command, Vietnam Agencies on personnel matters of the Marine Advisory Unit and the Vietnamese Marine Corps.

2. Reports received from the Vietnamese Marine Corps generally dictate those areas requiring advisory assistance.

3. Reports and reporting procedures of primary interest to the G-1 Advisor are as follows:

   a. Joint Table of Distribution Changes

     (1) The Joint Table of Distribution is a MACV published document which prescribes the numbers, grades and MOSs of the U.S. personnel within each unit of MACV, including the Marine Advisory Unit.

     (2) Additional personnel requirements are completely justified by letter to Chief, Naval Advisory Group, who in turn submits the proposal to the Commander, U.S. Military Assistance Command, Vietnam for approval. Upon approval, the request is published as a revision to the Joint Table of Distribution and forwarded simultaneously to Commander in Chief, Pacific and Joint Chief of Staff for final approval and implementation.

   b. TO&E Review

     (1) The TO&E review for the Vietnamese Marine Corps is accomplished when directed by the Senior Marine Advisor but not less than once every two years.

     (2) The G-1 Advisor's primary interest is to ascertain that the appropriate number of personnel is provided based on the mission, equipment and organization. This review is accomplished by the Staff of the Marine Advisory Unit under the cognizance of the G-3 Advisor.

     (3) After the review, the final review is accomplished by a combined compromised of Vietnamese Marine Corps Staff Officer and U.S. Marine Corps Advisor.

     (4) The Vietnamese Marine Corps' procedures and responsibilities for preparation/revisions of TO&E are attached as TAB A.

   c. Strength Reporting (QD 22).

     (1) The Strength Report is prepared at the unit level (battalions and separate companies) of the Vietnamese Marine Corps and reflects the assigned strength, plus any attachments, and minus those personnel sick, TAD, UA, deserters, away at school, or temporarily absent from their reporting unit for any other reason. The report contains basically the same information as the Unit Dairy of the U.S. Marine Corps.

(2) The report is designed to:

(a) Simplify strength reporting procedures to coincide with present RVNAF organization and personnel administration policies.

(b) Provide the Joint General Staff, RVNAF with accurate information of the overall strength of RVNAF forces.

(c) Help responsible command levels control unit strength capabilities and understand the morale of subordinate personnel.

(d) Provide data related to the strength development and service status unit personnel.

(3) A copy of each Strength Report prepared is furnished the Marine Advisory Unit (G-1 Advisor). From this report, the G-1 Advisor provides input to the G-3 Advisor for preparation of the SEER, RIMS, and the Weekly Summary reports. Additionally, he prepares himself for one quarterly MACV personnel conferences and frequent discussion with MACV J-1 concerning the personnel status of the Vietnamese Marine Corps.

(4) Procedures for the preparation and forwarding of the Strength Report are contained in the 24 May 1967 translation of RVNAF Directive 530-2 dated 1 January 1967.

d. RVNAF Improvement and Modernization Management Systems (RIMS).

(1) This classified report is published quarterly by MACV to provide the Commander, U.S. Military Assistance Command, Vietnam, the Chief, RVNAF Joint General Staff, and MACV and JGS sections and agencies with information on the status of RVNAF and the progress of the expansion, improvement, and modernization program for the Vietnamese Armed Forces.

(2) The content of RIMS is derived from statistical data provided MACV agencies. Although some of the data is obtained from U. S. Advisory channels, most of the data is obtained directly from Vietnamese sources.

(3) The RIMS is designed to provided COMUSMACV and the Chief, RVNAF Joint General Staff with information on the status of RVNAF and the progress of major programs supporting the expansion, improvement and modernization of areas of weakness which require attention of high level commanders. The system concentrates on the areas of personnel, training, and logistics, and attempts to portray both the areas of weakness and the status of actions required for their correction. By highlighting areas in which corrective action is lagging behind the program, command decisions can be made and appropriate directives issued.

(4) The system is intended to improve the management of available resources by both MACV and RVNAF Joint General Staff, and to measure the rate of improvement in the

capability of RVNAF. The ultimate goal is for the data required for support of the system to flow through RVNAF channels so that the Joint General Staff will be capable of employing the system independent of MACV participation or assistance.

(5) Evaluation of operations is included to the extent necessary to determine whether the operational effectiveness of RVNAF improve as the capabilities of the force are improved as a result of expansion, improvement and modernization. Overall MACV evaluation of operational effectiveness will continue to be made through the SEER system. Detailed information on preparation and submission of the SEER is covered in Marine Advisory Unit Order 3480.1.

(6) Standards or goals have been established for most indicators included in the system. Wherever possible, these standards have been established on three levels - desired, satisfactory, unsatisfactory - to permit measurement of progress and improvement as well as identification of weakness. The standards used are, wherever possible, those which have previously been established by JGS or recommended by MACV. In cases where goals or standards have no yet been established, previous performance serves as a basis for comparison. No direct comparison, in the sense that one unit is better that another, is intended, nor are units ranked.

e. Weekly Summary.

(1) Input for the Weekly Summary will be prepared and submitted to the G-3 Advisor not later that 1600 of each Thursday. The report will include but not limited to, the following information.

(a) Recruiting. Number of personnel recruited for the reporting period can be obtained on or about the 3d and 18th of each month from the Assistant Chief of Staff, G-1, Vietnamese Marine Corps.

(b) Desertion. The desertion rate may be obtained from either, the Strength Report (QD 22) or directly from the Assistant Chief of Staff, G-1 at the same times as the recruiting figures are obtained.

(c) Promotions. Prepared and submitted at such times as the Promotion Board meets normally the first of each quarter. Rank imbalances, in any should be indicated.

(d) Miscellaneous. Include any comments relevant to dependent housing, schools, PX, commissaries, etc.

CHAPTER IV
PART II: AWARDS PROGRAM

4200   SUBMISSION OF AWARD RECOMMENDATIONS

1. Marine Advisory Unit personnel recommending Vietnamese Marines or U. S. Marine Advisor personnel for U.S. Awards must comply with Marine Advisory Unit Order 1650.1.

2. Upon approval of the award by the Senior Marine Advisor, it is forwarded to the Commander, Naval Forces, Vietnam.

3. If approved, the recommendation will be forwarded to or via the Commander, U.S. Military Assistance Command, Vietnam to secure U.S. Mission concurrence if for Vietnamese Marines. If concurrence is obtained, the award is either returned or forwarded to the awarding authority, depending upon the type of award recommended.

4201   APPROVAL OF AWARDS

1. The Commander, U.S. Naval Forces, Vietnam has authority to approve award recommendations of all types up to and including the Bronze Star Medal. All other recommendations must be forwarded to higher authority for approval.

4202   PRESENTATION OF AWARDS

1. Upon receipt of the approved award the Marine Advisory Unit, the Awards Officer, Vietnamese Marine Corps will be notified. The Awards Officer will make arrangements for an appropriate ceremony for the presentation.

CHAPTER IV
PART III: PUBLIC AFFAIRS ADVISOR

4300   PUBLIC AFFAIRS OFFICER (PAO) BRIEFING

1. The G-1 Advisor in his capacity as PAO Advisor briefs each incoming advisor concerning the Vietnamese Marine Corps' informational service program and its function. The briefing includes current policies and guidelines for field advisors in dealing with the Free World Press corps and representatives of military informational services.

2. A brief interview with each incoming advisor provides information for use in a hometown news release concerning the new advisor's arrival at the Marine Advisory Unit.

4301   BIOGRAPHICAL FILES

1. A file folder containing biographical information and current photographs is maintained in the admin office for each advisor. Copies of photographs of the advisor and other personal data concerning the advisor will be retained in the file. Complete files are available to advisors upon completion of their tour of duty with the Marine Advisory Unit.

4302   PHOTOGRAPHY

1. The Administrative Officer provides limited photographic service for the Marine Advisory Unit with all processing and finishing done through the NAVFORV Photographic Laboratory. Types of photographic services available are:

    a. Photo Board Identification Pictures. The Administrative Officer arranges for portrait photos of all incoming advisors. Extra finished photos and negatives are held on file in the individual's personal folder.

    b. Driver's License Photographs. The Motor Transport Advisor obtains two suitable polaroid photographs of each incoming advisor.

    c. Hometown News Releases.

    (1) News releases prepared by the PAO Advisor are forwarded to the hometown newspapers of each incoming advisor with appropriate photographs. In addition, news releases with photographs are forwarded when advisors are decorated, promoted or otherwise involved in a newsworthy event.

    (2) News releases of a hometown nature concerning individual advisors are not forwarded without the consent of the advisor concerned.

4303   PRESS PHOTOGRAPHY

1. The Administrative Officer arranges for photographic coverage of suitable news events and ceremonies. Once processed by the NAVFORV photographic laboratory, finished prints are distributed by the PAO to news media, as applicable; to the individuals concerned or filed in the PA office.

2. All negatives are returned from the photographic laboratory with proof sheets and are filed in the PAO office.

4304   FILM SUPPLY

1. The NAVFORV Photographic Laboratory provides 8 rolls of 35mm B&W film and 4 rolls of color slide film once each month. The film is usually picked up on the first day of each month.

4305   NEWS MEDIA RELATIONSHIPS

1. The PAO Advisor assists the VNMC ISO as an English-speaking counterpart and frequently assists in contacting and transporting representatives of the Saigon Press Corps to events warranting new coverage as concerning the Vietnamese Marine Corps.

2. In order to cultivate press contacts, the PAO Advisor attends, when possible, the Joint Vietnamese MACV Press Briefing sponsored by the Joint U.S. Public Affairs Office.

3. The PAO Advisor also works closely with the Information Advisory Division of the MACV Information Office in matters of contact with civilian and military press representatives.

4. The PAO Advisor, with a representative of the VMC ISO, accompanies all press representatives visiting or otherwise covering units, functions or events connected with the Vietnamese Marine Corps.

4306   MONTHLY NEWSLETTER

1. The PAO Advisor publishes a monthly newsletter, The "CO-VAN" for the information and entertainment of the members and former members of the Marine Advisory Unit.

2. The CO-VAN is rough-typed and deadline by the PAO Advisor and submitted for approval to the Assistant Senior Marine Advisor.

3. Once approved, the copy is typed on multi-lith mats by the Marine Advisory Unit administrative section and copy read by the PAO Advisor upon completion

4. Printing is accomplished by the NAVFORV Reproduction Section.

. Final distribution is made by the administrative section of the Marine Advisory Unit using a distribution list provided by the PAO Advisor.

6. The CO-VAN is an official USMC publication printed in accordance with Marine Corps Order P5600.31. It is printed on the 30th of each month.

STANDING OPERATING PROCEDURES FOR MARINE ADVISORY UNIT

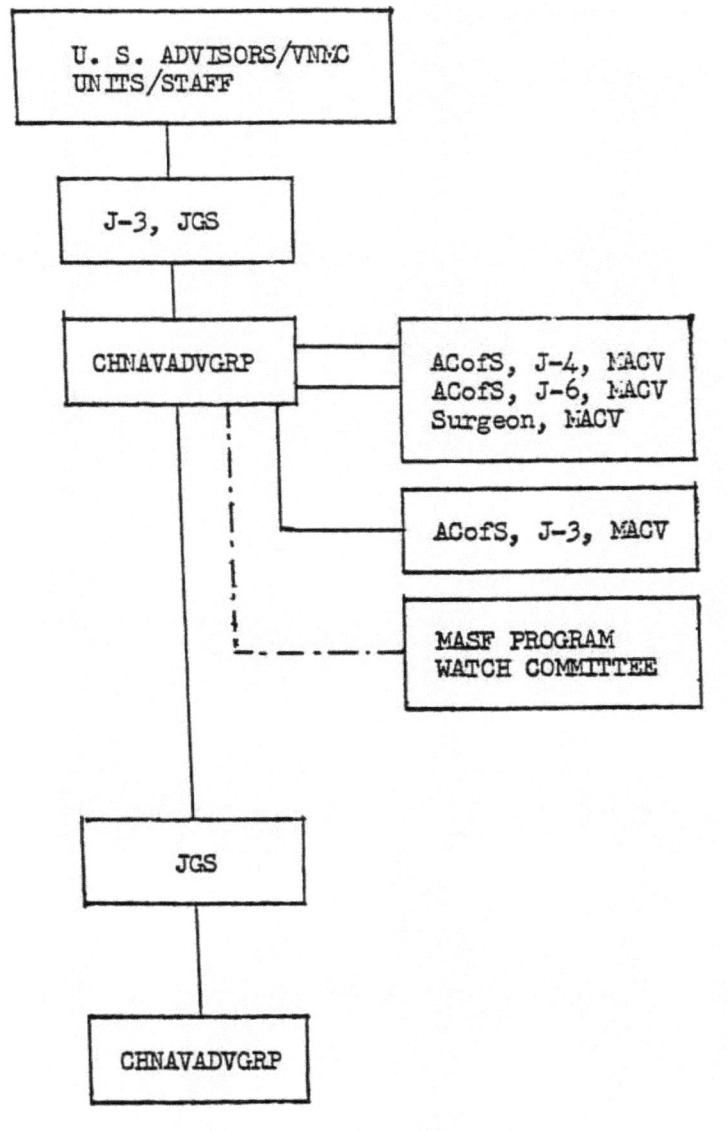

1. Develop and/or revise draft TO&E and T/A.

1. Review.
2. Forward 7 copies to CHNAVADVGRP.

1. Review (including techical review by MACV staff agencies for RVNAF common equipment.
2. Approval of draft TO&E.
3. Program increase requires Watch Committee approval.

1. Publication.

1. Authentication for programming and budgeting.
2. Distribution to staff and U. S. Advisors.

TAB A -- VNMC PROCEDURES AND RESPONSIBILITIES FOR TO&E

1. The Vietnamese Marine Corps is to originate the draft in coordination with appropriate advisors and submit through RVNAF service channels to the J-3, Joint General Staff.

2. After review, the J-3, Joint General Staff, is to forward seven bilingual copies of the draft TO&E, revision, or change to the Chief, Naval Advisory Group for review and approval. Section III of the Vietnamese Marine Corps TO&E, containing common items of equipment monitored by RVNAF technical services are to be submitted to the Assistant Chief of Staff, J-4, MACV; Assistant Chief of Staff, J-6, MAVC; and Command Surgeon, MAVC, prior to final review and approval. The Assistant Chief of Staff, MA, MACV, is also to coordinate the TO&E with the Assistant Chief of Staff, J-3, MACV.

3. Subsequently to review and approval, Chief, Naval Advisory Group is to enter all adjustments in red on the draft master work copy and deliver to the Chief, Joint General Staff, with a recommendation to publish. Chief, Naval Advisory Group total processing time is not to exceed 30 working days.

4. After printing, the Chief, Joint General Staff, is to forward 30 copies of the TO&E or change to Chief, Naval Advisory Group for proofreading and authentication.

5. Chief, Naval Advisory Group is to enter proofreading corrections in red, authenticate, and distribute TO&E or changes as follows:

   a. CINPAC, 1 copy

   b. J-3, JGS, 2 copies.

   c. ACofS, MA, MACV, 5 copies

   d. ACofS, J-4, MACV, 1 copy (when appropriate).

   e. CINCUSARPAC, 1 copy (when appropriate).

   f. Command Surgeon, MACV, 1 copy.

6. The J-3, Joint General Staff is responsible for the RVNAF distribution of TO&E. The Chief, Naval Advisory Group is to accomplish Naval Advisory Group distribution.

7. A complete review of the TO&E is to be conducted on a two year cycle. However, changes or revisions are to be requested at any time the need arises.

CHAPTER V

1. To be issued at a later date. [not in the original document]

CHAPTER VI
G-3 ADVISORY ELEMENT

PART I   ORGANIZATION   PARAGRAPH

INTERNAL ORGANIZATION FOR GARRISON OPERATIONS 6100

INTERNAL ORGANIZATION FOR FIELD OPERATIONS 6101

SPECIFIC TASKS 6102

PART II   ADMINISTRATION

BRIEFING OF INCOMING ADVISORS 6200

G-3 READING FILE 6201

REPORTING 6202

CHAPTER VI
PART I: ORGANIZATION

6100   INTERNAL ORGANIZATION FOR GARRISON OPERATIONS

1. The internal organization, with the G-3 Advisory Element, when operating in garrison, is shown below.

2. The basic concept of daily operations within the G-3 Advisory Element is to have the Assistant G-3 Advisor manage the office; he is supported by the Operations Chief. At the same time the other advisors will be working directly with their counterparts as much as possible.

3. All advisors under the cognizance of the G-3 Advisor will maintain desktop procedures and continuity files and keep themselves abreast on all G-3 Advisor areas to allow continuity during periods of leave, R&R and unit advisor refill when needed.

4. The G-3 Advisor will maintain close contact with unit advisors in order to ensure close coordination and execution of Senior Marine Advisor directives.

6101   INTERNAL ORGANIZATION FOR FIELD OPERATIONS

1. The internal organization, with the G-3 Advisory element, when conducting field operation, is shown below.

2. The Assistant Training Command Advisor will function as the G-3 watch officer. The Training Advisor will assume additional duties as a Division Liaison Officer. In addition, the Division Artillery Advisor will function as the FSCC Advisor under the cognizance of the G-3 Advisor.

6102   SPECIFIC TASKS

1. Chapter II, Part II, of the SOP discusses Billet Incumbent Tasks.

CHAPTER VI
PART II: ADMINISTRATION

6200 BRIEFING OF INCOMING ADVISORS

1. The G-3 Advisor is assigned the responsibility of ensuring proper indoctrination of incoming advisors in the following subject areas:

    a. VNMC History, Organization, Mission, Combat Proficiency

    b. MAU Organization

    c. Current Deployment of VNMC; Future Deployment

    d. VNMC Training

    e. POL/PSY Warfare

    f. Riverine and Airmobile Operations

    g. Familiarization with Command and Control Helicopters

    h. SITREP, SPOTREPs, Combat After Action Reports and Monthly and Quarterly SEER Reports

2. The briefing on those subject areas will be completed prior to advisor assignment.

6201 G-3 READING FILE

1. A reading file is maintained within the G-3 Advisory Element which permits the unit advisors to update themselves with the overall Vietnam situation.

6202 REPORTING

1. The following operation and recurring reports are required as indicated:

Report	Due	Ref
a. Admiral's Memorandum.	Weekly	Verbal
b. Memorandum to Asst Chief of Staff	Weekly	Verbal
c. SEER (Quarterly Effectiveness Report).	Quarterly	MACV Dir 335-1

d. LOP (Monthly Measure out of Progress).	Monthly	MACV Dir 335-13
e. MOP (Quarterly Measurement of Progress).	Quarterly	MACV Dir 335-22

Report	Due	Ref
f. Monthly Historical Summary.	Monthly	MCO -P5750.1B
g. VIPREP (Vietnamization Progress Report).	Semi-annually	NAVFORV INST 5200.20
h. RVNAF Improvement and Modernization Program Progress Report	Quarterly	MACV Dir 335-28
i. TOMMS (Training Objectives Measurements Management System Report).	Quarterly	MACV Dir 350-3(chl)

CHAPTER VII
G-4 ADVISORY ELEMENT

| **PART I** | **GENERAL** | **PARAGRAPH** |

ORGANIZATION 7100

GENERAL DUTIES 7101

MILITARY ASSISTANCE SERVICE FUNDED PROGRAM 7102

ANNUAL MASF INVENTORY 7103

O&MA COMMON ITEMS 7104

REVIEW OF PRIOR YEAR MASF PROGRAMS 7105

BRIEFING OF INCOMING ADVISORS 7106

G-4 READING FILE 7107

PART II   SUPPLY ADVISOR

GENERAL 7200

RECEIPT OF USMC DELIVERED MASF EQUIPMENT 7201

INVENTORY AND T/E STATUS CARDS 7202

ANNUAL MASF INVENTORY 7203

MARINE ADVISORY UNIT SUPPLY SUPPORT 7204

PART III   MOTOR TRANSPORT

GENERAL 7300

MAINTENANCE 7301

SPARE PARTS 7302

INSPECTIONS 7303

TRAINING 7304

TROOP AND EQUIPMENT MOVEMENTS 7305

MILITARY ASSISTANCE SERVICE FUNDED (MASF) ASSETS 7306

ADVISOR VEHICLES 7307

MAINTENANCE AND REPAIR OF ADVISOR VEHICLES 7308

MOTOR TRANSPORT ADVISOR TECHNIQUES 7309

PART IV   COMMUNICATIONS

GENERAL 7400

MAINTENANCE 7401

COMMUNICATION SECURITY 7402

FREQUENCY ASSIGNMENTS 7403

CALL SIGNS 7404

RADIO SET CHARACTERISTICS AND ANTENNAS 7405

COMMUNICATION ADVISOR STAFF RESPONSIBILITIES 7406

PART V   ENGINEER

GENERAL 7500

VNMC ENGINEER BATTALION 7501

FORCE CIVIL ENGINEER, NAVFORV 7502

RECEIPT/ISSUE OF U.S. FURNISHED MATERIALS 7503

OICC - PLANS AND PROGRAM 7504

ROICC - RESIDENT OFFICERS-IN-CHARGE CONSTRUCTION 7505

MAP SUPPLY FOR MAU ADVISORS 7506

MAU BUILDING MAINTENANCE 7507

MASF PROGRAM 7508

PART VI   SPECIAL SERVICES

GENERAL 7600

SPECIAL SERVICES SUPPORT 7601

REQUISITIONING OF SPECIAL SERVICES EQUIPMENT 7602

INTERNAL SUPPLY PROCEDURES 7603

REPORTS 7604

CHAPTER VII
PART I: GENERAL

7100   ORGANIZATION

1. The G-4 (Logistics) Advisory Element consists of the G-4 Advisor, Senior Medical Advisor, Medical Service Advisor, Supply Advisor, Communication Advisor, Engineer and Assistant Engineer Advisors, Motor Transport Advisor and Ordnance Advisor. The organizational structure of the G-4 Advisory Element is as follows.

7101   GENERAL DUTIES

1. The G-4 Advisor is the principal Marine Advisor to the Assistant Chief of Staff G-4, Vietnamese Marine Corps. This responsibility includes advising the G-4, Vietnamese Marine Corps, in matters pertaining to supply, evacuation and hospitalization, transportation, service, communications, engineer, ordnance and maintenance assistance. Additionally, the G-4 Advisor will coordinate the Military Assistance Service Funded Program and Tables of Equipment for the Vietnamese Marine Corps. The G-4 Advisor will also function as the Marine Advisory Unit S-4 Officer. The G-4 Advisor staff responsibilities for the above tasks are as follows:

   a. Supply

      (1) Planning, coordinating and supervising all supply functions.

      (2) Planning and supervising the procuring, storing, distributing and security of supplies.

      (3) Establishing priorities and allocations for regulated items.

      (4) Coordinating with the G-3 Advisor the establishing of priorities for material in short supply.

      (5) Planning and supervising the collection and disposing of surplus, excess, salvage, and captured supplies.

      (6) Supervising property accounting.

      (7) Planning, coordinating and supervising the Military Assistance Service Funded Program.

   b. Evacuation and Hospitalization

      (1) Planning and supervising the evacuation of sick, injured and wounded.

(2) Coordinating with the G-1 Advisor and G-3 Advisor to determine requirements for the evacuation and hospitalization of sick, injured, and wounded prisoners of war and civilians.

(3) Coordinating with the G-1 Advisor and the G-3 Advisor to determine requirements for hospitalization and evacuation based upon casualties sustained.

c. Transportation

(1) Planning for non tactical troop movements.

(2) Planning for the transportation of units, personnel and supplies by land, water and air.

(3) Arranging for ground traffic regulations and control.

d. Service

(1) Recommending the organization and equipment of the combat support units and the allocation, movement and employment of these units.

(2) Planning for the maintenance and repair of supplies and equipment.

(3) Planning, coordinating and supervising construction of all facilities except fortifications and tactical communications.

(4) Planning for the maintenance and repair of utilities and facilities.

e. Engineer

(1) Prepare plans for the construction, repair and maintenance of VNMC facilities including base camps, the hospital, training center, supply installation, and traffic routes using MILCON funds.

(2) Plans for the construction and renovation of Dependent Shelters.

(3) Develops, prepares and supervises the execution of engineer technical training program.

(4) Supervises the determination of requirements for programming, requisitioning, procurement, storage, distribution, security, and documentation of engineer equipment and supplies.

(5) Plans and supervises such activities as selection of sites for the establishment of supply dumps, unloading points, aid and medical clearing sections, and related facilities, both at fire support bases and at helicopter landing zones.

f. <u>Miscellaneous Related Subjects</u>
(1) Supervising all administrative functions in logistic matter including the preparation of logistical studies, estimates, records and reports; and the preparation, authentication and distribution of administrative plans and orders.

7102   MILITARY ASSISTANCE SERVICE FUNDED PROGRAM

1. The U.S. Marine Corps is tasked with the responsibility of providing major end items of equipment to the Vietnamese Marine Corps. The Commander in Chief, Pacific supplement to the DOD Military Assistance Manual (CSMAM) sets forth procedures to be followed for the Military Assistance Service Program.
2. The RVNAF is tasked with the responsibility of providing Class I, III, IV, V and Class II common service support items to the VNMC. The RVNAF is also responsible for partial third echelon and all higher echelon maintenance support.

3. The G-4, in conjunction with other staff advisors, must determine the major items of equipment required by the VNMC and incorporate these requirements into the MASF program.

4. The MASF program is submitted via NAVFORV and MAVC to the Commanding General, Fleet Marine Force, Pacific by 1 February of each year. The program consists of requirements for three subsequent fiscal years. The current fiscal year programs updated quarterly. The basis for the program submission is the annual MASF inventory and T/A changes (to include force structure increase and improvement modernization programs. The MASF program is formed into two parts; initial investment costs (to fill allowances and attrition cost (based on actual usage history).

7103   <u>ANNUAL MASF INVENTORY</u>

1. The G-4 Advisor commencing in June of each year shall conduct an annual inventory of all items received from the United States Government. All Vietnamese Marine Corps units will be visited and the equipment inventoried and inspected for serviceability.

2. The results of the inventory will be recorded on the Inventory Requisition and T/E Status Cards by using unit.

7104   <u>O&MA COMMON ITEMS</u>

1. The U.S. Army/RVNAF is tasked with providing common service support to the VNMC. A common service support item is an item listed in the U.S. Army Supply Bulletin 700-20 with a Procuring Appropriation Code "2" or "3" or as designed by MACV/CLC directives.

2. Requirements for these items will be determined by the G-4 Advisor, in conjunction with other staff advisors, and will be submitted to MACV (MACMAPR) on Format E's. Instructions for completing Format E's are described in the CSMAM.

7105   REVIEW OF PRIOR YEAR MASF PROGRAMS

1. The G-4 Advisor will continually review the status of all outstanding prior year MASF requisitions. This can be accomplished through liaison with U. S. Navy Military Assistance Service Funded Plans and Program Officer, and Headquarters, U.S. Marine Corps (Code AO4G).

   a. Monthly:

      (1) MACV Major Items of Equipment Received Report

      (2) CMC VNMC Logistics Information

   b. Quarterly:

      (1) VNMC in Use Weapons Density List.

      (2) RVNAF Improvement and Modernization Program Progress Report.

7106   BRIEFING OF INCOMING ADVISORS

1. Marine Advisory Unit Order 1500.1 directs the G-4 Advisor to ensure proper indoctrination of incoming advisors in the following subject areas:

   a. G-4 Advisor Element and duties

   b. Military Assistance Service Funded Program.

   c. RVNAF Logistical System.

2. The G-4 Advisor will additionally coordinate briefings by the following special staff officers to incoming advisors:

   a. Supply

   b. Medical

   c. Communication

   d. Engineer

e. Motor Transport

f. Ordnance

7107 G-4 READING FILE

1. A current reading file containing all aspects of logistical information within the Republic of Vietnam is maintained in the G-4 Advisor's office. This file is available to each advisor.

CHAPTER VII
PART II: SUPPLY ADVISOR

7200 GENERAL

1. The Supply Advisor performs the general duties of a special staff officer under the staff cognizance of the G-4 Logistics Advisor, with respect to general supply matters. The Supply Advisor staff responsibilities include:

    a. Planning, coordinating, and supervising the acquisitions, storage, control, security, issue, recovery, and redistribution of all supplies and equipment.

    b. Furnishing advice and information relative to supply procedures, including property accounting, property responsibility, and standardization of material.

2. The Supply Advisor, in addition to the Supply Advisor to the Vietnamese Marine Corps, must maintain liaison with other units, i.e., NAVFORV, MSTS, 4th TC, VNNSC, 3rd ALC, MACV, NSA, ICCV, USARV, HQ Saigon Support Command and 624th S&S Co.

3. The Supply Advisor is also the Assistant G-4 Logistics Advisor.

7201 RECEIPT OF USMC DELIVERED MASF EQUIPMENT

1. The Supply Advisor will receive, inspect and receipt for all material requisitioned through the Military Assistance Service Funded Program. The material received from the U.S. source will normally be accepted at the Vietnamese Naval Supply Center. Material may also be received at Newport, and Tan Son Nhut. In transferring U.S. property to the Vietnamese Marine Corps, the Commanding Officer in the case of communication equipment or theft representatives will provide the Supply Advisor with a receipt of delivery.

7202 INVENTORY AND T/E STATUS CARDS

1. The Supply Advisor will maintain an Inventory and T/E Status Card on each item of Military Assistance Service Funded support material. This card will indicate the item name, FSN, MASF price and allowance for each unit and the quantity on hand for the using unit.

7203 ANNUAL MASF INVENTORY

1. The MASF inventory will be conducted commencing the 2d Quarter of each Fiscal Year. All government provided materials will be inventoried and imported for use and maintenance.

2. The Vietnamese Marine Corps, G-4, will determine the schedule for the inventory.

3. During the annual MASF inventory all U.S. Government supplied equipment will be inspected for serviceability. A report from each Technical Staff Advisor on the condition of the equipment will be prepared for the Assistant Senior Marine Advisor.

7204 MARINE ADVISORY UNIT SUPPLY SUPPORT

1. All individual equipment will be issued at the MACV Central Issue Facility. Replacement items will be exchanged or replaced at the Direct Support Unit at Long Binh by the Supply Advisor and issued to the individual advisor.

2. The Supply Advisor will coordinate the procurement of all advisor uniforms, berets and insignia. The Supply Advisor will maintain two (2) extra uniform trousers in the MAU storeroom for each field advisor. These uniforms will be procured through use of the AIK Fund. Berets and embroidered insignia will be paid for by the individual advisor.

3. The Supply Advisor will utilize the MACV authorized Self-Service Supply Center and will provide consumable supplies on an as required basis.

4. A minimum of 40 cases of rations will be maintained for emergency use. The rations will be stored and rotated as per current MACV Directives.

5. A sufficient supply of ammunition will be maintained for emergency use and/or advisor resupply. An inventory will be conducted quarterly and the results forwarded to the Assistant Senior Marine Advisor.

6. The Supply Advisor will also be appointed the Property Book Officer and will establish an organizational property book. This property book will be established on a DA Form 14-110 and the Property Book Officer is responsible for keeping the original and duplicate files of hand receipts current and will maintain a separate document register on DA Form 2064.

7. The supply Officer maintains a plant account of Navy property on charge to this unit from NAVFORV to support the administrative requirements associated with the Senior Marine Advisor's function as Special Assistant for Marine Affairs to COMNAVFORV. These plant account records are maintained by the Field Services Supply Office, NSA.

CHAPTER VII
PART III: MOTOR TRANSPORT

7300 <u>GENERAL</u>

1. This directive is applicable to the Motor Transport Advisor, Marine Advisory Unit. It is intended to amplify duties of the Motor Transport Advisor, to set forth general organization of the Vietnamese Marine Corps, outline operation, maintenance and training procedures of the Vietnamese Marine Corps motor transport, and to define the advisor vehicle program.

2. The Motor Transport Advisor provides advice and assistance to the Vietnamese Marine Corps in all aspects of transportation, with emphasis on motor transport. Additionally he functions as a special staff officer to the Senior Marine Advisor for matters pertaining to motor transport.

3. The Vietnamese Marine Corps Division Transportation Officer has overall staff cognizance for the operation and maintenance management of all motor transport equipment. Additionally, he coordinates all nonorganic air, land, and sea transportation support provided from sources external to the VNMC. The Division Transportation Officer is the Motor Transport Advisor's primary counterpart. Accordingly, good rapport and daily contact must be maintained if meaningful, timely advice and assistance is to be rendered. Additionally, the Motor Transport Advisor will find it necessary to work closely with the Division Logistics Officer, Supply Officer, and G-4 in order to assure coordinated advice is provided on receipt, storage, distribution, documentation of repair parts, and external maintenance support of motor transport equipment.

4. The Commanding Officer, Transportation Company, Marine Division is the Motor Transport Advisor's secondary counterpart. The Transportation Company is a separate company within the VNMC Division, and approximates the size of a USMC FMF Motor Transport Battalion. The Transportation Company is capable of providing a one-time lift of three infantry battalions by truck.

7301 <u>MAINTENANCE</u>

1. Maintenance is the care and servicing of equipment and facilities by selected personnel for the purpose of maintaining it in a satisfactory operating condition. This provides for systematic inspection, detection and the subsequent repair of failures before they occur or before they develop into major defects.

2. Using VNMC units perform 1st and 2nd echelon maintenance on all motor transport equipment assigned. Maintenance and repairs authorized for their levels of maintenance are set forth in JGS/RVNAF directives.

3. The unit commander is responsible for the management, support, logistics and training of personnel within the unit's maintenance programs.

4. Each infantry and artillery battalion plus Headquarters Battalion, Amphibious Support Battalion, Medical Battalion, Transportation Company, Engineer Battalion, Communications Company, and Training Center has a motor transport facility, tools, test equipment, and personnel capable of performing second echelon maintenance on authorized equipment. Advisory effort must include the proper operation and maintenance of all vehicles plus proper utilization of tools, and monitoring training of drivers and mechanics. Requisitioning procedures and repair parts stock levels should be periodically checked by advisors.

5. Third echelon maintenance for the VNMC is provided by ARVN Ordnance Direct Support Companies. These are referred to as "DSUs" and are located throughout the Republic of Vietnam. ARVN procedures for utilization of the ARVN maintenance program.

6. Occasionally, it will be necessary for a VNMC unit to request maintenance support from the DSU's Mobile Repair Team due to location of the VNMC unit, condition of the equipment or the availability of work space at the DSU.

7302   <u>SPARE PARTS</u>

1. The advisor must familiarize himself with authorized channels within the VNMC plus external RVNAF support for the procurement and programming of spare parts. Liaison must be maintained with U.S. Army advisors to DSUs and Ordnance Support Battalions in order to solicit information for effective monitoring of this program.

2. All repair parts and publications are requisitioned by individual VNMC battalions and separate companies directly from their assigned supporting DSU. Particular emphasis must be placed on the maintenance and storage of repair parts reflected on the Parts Load Lists (PLL) for each type vehicle. Storage of spare parts is important and should provide for adequate protection, preservation, and ready identification. Each VNMC unit authorized a second echelon maintenance capability is required to maintain a stockage of spare parts based on the PLL. Selective interchange of vehicle components, commonly referred to as cannibalization, is to be discouraged.

3. Each DSU operates a Direct Exchange (DX) program for in-kind exchange of repairable subassemblies such as generators, regulators, starting motors, wheel cylinders, master cylinders, etc. If a replacement is not immediately available at the DSU the unserviceable item will be returned immediately available at the DSU the unserviceable item will be turned in for repair or rebuild and receipt provided the customer. When the work is completed the item will be returned.

4. Each VNMC battalion and separate company is assigned a specific DSU for support, depending on the unit's geographic location. The DSUs receive work orders and requisitions

directly from the VNMC battalion or separate company. DSUs providing full time support for VNMC units in the Saigon/Thu Duc area are listed below:

    a. The 831st Ordnance Direct Support Company, located across the Bien Hoa Highway from the road to Thu Duc, supports the 1st, 2nd, 3rd, 5th, 6th, 7th, 8th, and 9th Infantry Battalions, 1st, 2nd, and 3rd Artillery Battalions, Training Center, Medical Battalion Communications Company and Engineer Battalion.

    b. The 833rd Ordnance Direct Support Company, located near Bien Hoa, support the 4th Infantry Battalion at Vung Tau. This support is accomplished by a maintenance section from the 833rd also located at Vung Tau.

    c. The 835th Ordnance Direct Support Company, located in Saigon, supports Headquarters Battalion, Service Battalion, and Transportation Company.

    d. The Ordnance Direct Support Companies are in turn supported by the 230th Ordnance Support Battalion. This unit furnishes 4th echelon maintenance to all VNMC units plus provides all second and third echelon repair parts to the DSUs. Direct liaison with U.S. Army advisors to the 230th is often necessary to solve maintenance or repair parts problems encountered at individual DSUs.

7303   <u>INSPECTIONS</u>

1. The Motor Transport Advisor should accompany the Division Transportation Officer, or his representative, on technical inspections of motor transport equipment, records, maintenance, and personnel. Although the Motor Transport Advisor is not the inspector, he will be able to obtain a great deal of information to guide him in his duties.

7304   <u>TRAINING</u>

1. Advising the Division Transportation Officer on maintaining and supervising a technical training program for drivers and mechanics is an important role of the Motor Transport Advisor. This requires close liaison with the G-3 Training Advisor in respect to schools and procurement of training aids.

    a. There are two principal schools available for motor transport training:

    (1) The RVNAF Transportation School:

    (a) Located at Camp Le Loi, Quang Trung location, approximately 14 kilometers NW of Saigon on Route 1.

    (b) The school is divided into two main courses, one for drivers and one for mechanics. The driver's training includes classroom instruction and practical application phases on driving and driver's maintenance. The mechanic's training consists of classroom and practical application training to qualify the mechanic in all phases of second echelon maintenance. The courses have been updated to correspond with the equipment modernization programs.

(c) Training aids are available at the school as well as copies of lesson outlines that can be incorporated into unit technical training. English copies of all lesson plans are available on a loan basis from the U.S. Army advisor of the school.

(2) The ARVN Ordnance School:

(a) Located in Camp Hanh Thong Tai in Go Vap District, approximately 7 kilometers from Tan Son Nhut.

(b) The school is the largest of its type in South Vietnam, offering an extensive variety of courses in weapons, ammunition and vehicular maintenance. The school offers courses for Officers, non-commissioned officers, and junior enlisted personnel in all branches of RVNAF.

b. Liaison visits are recommended as part of the in-processing for the Motor Transport Advisor.

7305 TROOP AND EQUIPMENT MOVEMENTS

1. Requests for troop and equipment moves beyond the organic capability of each unit are submitted to the VNMC Division G-4, Transportation Officer. Requirements are consolidated and forwarded to the RVNAF Officer. Requirements are consolidated and forwarded to the RVNAF Joint General Staff for assignment of fixed wing aircraft or ships. The Motor Transport Advisor must monitor this operation very closely from the time of request through completion of the move. When U. S. assets are involved such as aircraft or post facilities, the MTA must provide detailed coordination between U.S. agencies and the VNMC Transportation Officer. Requirements for ARVN vehicle support are submitted through command channels to the Area Logistic Command. Provisioning of vehicles is coordinated by the VNMC Transportation Officer.

7306 MILITARY ASSISTANCE SERVICE FUNDED (MASF) ASSETS

1. The Motor Transport Advisor must be familiar with the MASF program as it pertains to motor transport. An annual inventory of all MASF equipment is conducted by the MAU. This inventory is used as an opportunity to review the units' TO&E and recommend appropriate changes. It also can be employed as a media to evaluate unit motor transport operation, maintenance, and training. Notwithstanding this annual inventory, unit advisors are required to continuously monitor MASF material use, maintenance, storage, and security as part of their regular duties, and report to the Senior Marine Advisor any noted abuse or misuse of MASF support equipment.

7307   ADVISOR VEHICLES

1. The Vietnamese Marine Corps is authorized a number of vehicles, "For Advisor Use Only." These vehicles are in addition to the Vietnamese Marine Corps unit TO&Es. Current allowances of MAU advisor vehicles are established by MACV and set forth in MACV Directive 56-1.

   a. Assignment and distribution of advisor vehicles within the MAU is normally made by the Motor Transport Advisor in his capacity as Advisor Vehicle Coordinator, in concert with the G-4 Advisor.

   b. Requests for increases in the MAU advisor vehicle allowance are submitted directly to MACV in accordance with MACV Directive 56-1. The MACV "Watch Committee" will be convened to determine if the requests are sufficiently justified. The Motor Transport Advisor may be required to appear before the Watch Committee to further amplify on justification for request increases.

   c. When changing assignments of advisor vehicles within the MAU, the Vietnamese Marine Corps G-4 must be informed in order that arrangements can be made for correct Property Book accountability and maintenance support.

   d. Advisor vehicle drivers are provided by the unit to which the advisor is assigned. Any changes made in assigned drivers must be reported as soon as possible to the Motor Transport Advisor. Subsequently, a complete listing of advisor vehicles, advisor drivers, and advisor billet descriptions is furnished to the VNMC G-4 monthly by the Motor Transport Advisor. This listing is utilized by the VNMC to promulgate movement orders for assigned VNMC drivers and to verify Property Book accountability. Requests for reassignment of drivers for staff advisors will be submitted in writing to the VNMC Adjutant General. Field advisors will coordinate directly with their respective counterparts concerning any requested driver changes.

   e. The Motor Transport Advisor will issue U.S. Government Operators Permits and obtain Vietnamese Drivers' License for all MAU personnel required to operate VNMC vehicles in their performance of duty. Normally each advisor will be issued a U.S. Government and Vietnamese Driver's License during initial MAU in-processing. Additionally, each advisor is required to have written authorization from the Senior Marine advisor to operate VNMC vehicles.

7308   MAINTENANCE AND REPAIR OF ADVISOR VEHICLES

1. The VNMC is required by joint JGS/MACV directive to provide drivers maintenance, POL, and repair for advisor vehicles.

2. First echelon maintenance is the daily cleaning, adjustment and inspection of the vehicle plus checking oil, water, and battery fluid levels. If performed correctly and with regularity it will normally preclude more serious failures and ensure combat readiness of the advisors'

transportation media. First echelon maintenance is the responsibility of the driver. However, the individual advisor is required to ensure his assigned driver in fact performs thorough, timely, drivers' maintenance. Advisors will verify the quality of driver's maintenance performed on their vehicle by a weekly inspection utilizing the checklist provided in TABS D and E.

3. Second echelon maintenance and repair parts support of advisor vehicles is the responsibility of the unit to which the advisor is assigned. Brigade headquarters advisors and division staff advisors vehicles receive second echelon maintenance support from Headquarters Battalion Motor Transport Section. Individual advisors will ensure their advisor vehicle receives a second echelon lubrication (L1, L2 or Lq) and tune-up service from their unit motor pool each month.

4. Third echelon maintenance is the replacement of components and requires evacuation to the Ordnance Direct Support Company. This normally involves long periods of vehicle non-availability and can be prevented by insuring that proper first and second echelon maintenance is performed.

7309   MOTOR TRANSPORT ADVISOR TECHNIQUES

1. It is imperative to establish solid personal and professional rapport with your principal counterparts, the Division Transportation Officer and the Commanding Officer of Transportation Company. These officers should be aware of all projects you are working on and you should be available to assist them at all times.

2. Know the capabilities, limitations and maintenance procedures for all items of motor transport equipment authorized the VNMC. Learn proficient methods of inspecting each item. Generally, VNMC transportation officers are particularly well trained in the mechanical and maintenance aspects of vehicles, more so than U.S. officers of equal rank. In contrast, U.S. officers are generally more proficient in convoy operations, maintenance management, supply, procurement, and inspection techniques.

3. Become familiar with unit missions and capabilities plus authorization of personnel and equipment as set forth in TO&Es. Know the transportation officers and noncommissioned officers and after receiving permission from the Division Transportation Officer, visit unit shop areas and observe maintenance procedures. Appropriate recommendations should be made to the Division Transportation Officer.

4. Avoid becoming a supply system outside the Vietnamese channels. This merely leads to supply dependence on the advisor and inhibits effectiveness of the RVNAF "system." Remember that the advisor's mission is to upgrade the efficiency of the VNMC motor transport personnel and make them self-sufficient through their own maintenance and logistics system.

5. Where technically feasible offer two or three possible courses of action in making recom-

mendations to your counterparts. This avoids a strict "go" or "no go" situation allowing

the counterpart to adopt the course of action he feels will best get the job done within the VN culture and system.

6. Remember we are building a viable Vietnamese Marine Corps, based on the unique strengths and characteristics of RVN and its people. Equipment and procedures which are ideal for the U.S. Marine Corps may not be entirely appropriate for the VNMC.

7. Avoid developing detailed plans, programs, TO&Es, etc., unilaterally. A full and free interchange of ideas usually results in the best features of both you and your counterparts' ideas being implemented. You are and advisor, not an outsider. When something can be improved speak up and let it be known.

CHAPTER VII
PART IV: COMMUNICATIONS

7400 <u>GENERAL</u>

1. This directive is applicable to the Marine Advisory Unit. These procedures encompass the areas of Maintenance, Communications Security, Frequency Allocation, Call Signs, Communications Interference, Characteristic and Antenna Configuration.

7401 <u>MAINTENANCE</u>

1. Operator/first echelon maintenance is a user's responsibility. TAB A contains a prescribed maintenance checklist for radio sets.

   a. <u>Repair</u>. The Marine Advisory Unit has no organic maintenance capability. Therefore, advisor radios requiring maintenance shall use the following procedures for obtaining maintenance service.

      (1) Advisors in the immediate Saigon area obtain maintenance service through the Communications Advisor. Normally this can be accomplished on a "float" basis.

      (2) Advisors in remote areas should contact the nearest U.S. armed forces facility for repair. Most large maintenance facilities have a maintenance float capability where inoperative sets or components can be exchanged for operable sets. When an advisor's radio is exchanged from a maintenance float the new radio's serial number will be reported to the Communications Advisor.

      (3) The 536th Heavy Equipment Maintenance Company, U.S. Army, will provide maintenance for inoperable communications equipment. A complete work request, DA-2407, must accompany each separate item. The Naval Support Activity, Nha Be, may also be used for maintenance support, particularly for radio sets AN/GRC-106 and secure speech equipment. NSA, Nha Be has a "float" capability for the AN/GRC-106.

7402 <u>COMMUNICATION SECURITY</u>

1. Communication security principles must be adhered to by all advisors. In addition, advisors must be familiar with the content and use of the various Signal Operating Instructions (SOI)/Communications Operating Instructions (COI), numeral codes, authentication codes and operating codes employed by tactical control headquarters under which they are operating. In addition to instructions which may be contained in the SOI/COI, the following will be strictly adhered to:

   a. Do not encrypt friendly positions while in contact.

b. Do not encrypt enemy positions.

c. Enemy intercept capability increases as friendly transmissions increase; therefore, transmit only when necessary, avoid unauthorized procedures. Assume all transmissions are monitored unless speech secure equipment is employed.

d. In-house, locally produced codes are prohibited.

2. SOI/COI

a. One (1) updated copy is maintained by the Communications Advisor for use by the advisors.

3. Speech Secure Equipment

a. The use of speech secure equipment is encouraged when operating conditions permit.

7403 <u>FREQUENCY ASSIGNMENTS</u>

1. Frequencies are assigned to the MAU by COMNAVFORV.

2. Frequencies are assigned to the MAU by the Senior Advisor of the Headquarters to which the Vietnamese Marine Unit is under operational control. These frequencies are assigned out of a block of frequencies given to allied forces by the Vietnamese government. There are insufficient frequencies on the AN/PRC-25 (AN/PRC-77) band to provide clear communication at all times. Although efforts have been made on a geographical basis to avoid overlaps, because of atmospheric condition, pirating of frequencies by friendly and enemy units alike, occasionally two nets will be operating on the same frequency. Resolution of this problem will be the responsibility of the Senior Advisor present.

3. It is the responsibility of the Senior Advisor in the operational area to procure the current SOI, numeral, authentication and operational codes from the tactical control headquarters and to ensure that copies are distributed to the tactical unit advisor. The frequencies of U.S. supporting agencies in the area can be obtained from the SOI, to include the following:

a. Senior Headquarters

b. Adjacent units

c. Medical Evacuation Control

d. Artillery Support Unit

e. FAC Common

f. Helicopter Gunship Control

4. In the event of prolonged communications interference by a station not authorized to use the advisor frequency, the following information should be obtained and submitted to the Communications Advisor:

    a. Organization experiencing the interference

    b. Location

    c. Dates and times interference experienced

    d. Type of equipment affected

    e. Operating frequency affected

    f. Brief description of effects.
    g. Severity of interference.

    h. Call sign of station interfering.

    i. Fraction of 24-hour period interference occurred.

7404   CALL SIGNS

1. Marine Advisor Unit call signs are contained in the MAU SOI and are used for tactical/administrative traffic. Call signs of other U.S. units operating with in the area of Vietnamese Marine Corps units are contained in the SOI of the Controlling headquarters.

7405   RADIO SET CHARACTERISTICS AND ANTENNAS

1. An advisor must be familiar with the common radio sets in use throughout Vietnam. He should know the frequency range, operating range and compatibility of the various sets. To fully utilize his assets, an advisor should also be familiar with certain basic antennas and the capabilities of each type with the various radio sets. If necessary, the advisor should be qualified to construct appropriate field expedient antennas from available materials.

2. TAB B sets forth characteristics of radio sets most commonly used in country. TAB C provides details on antenna configuration for the RC-292 antenna when used with the AN/PRC-25 and AN/VRC-46 radio sets.

7406   COMMUNICATION ADVISOR STAFF RESPONSIBILITIES

1. The Marine Advisory Unit Communication Advisor's counterpart is the VNMC Division Communication-Electronics Officer. However, since Division Communications Company

Commander is co-located with the Division CEO the Communications Advisor can consider himself to have two counterparts.

2. The Communications Advisor provides advice and technical assistance to the Vietnamese Marine Corps on all matters pertaining to communications. Due to the classified nature of communication center and crypt function, only limited assistance can be offered. Assistance is hampered primarily due to lack of English translated publications and instructions.

3. The principal areas of involvement are technical training, maintenance, radio net and equipment, TO&E review and the MASF programming, and inventory. Each area is discussed below:

    a. <u>Technical training.</u> All Vietnamese Marine Corps technical training with the exception of on-the-job training is conducted at the RVNAF Signal School, Nung Tau, RVN. There is an "offshore" training program which provides quotas for students to attend the Radio Technicians and Operational Communication Officers Course, Quantico, Virginia. Information concerning these programs is maintained by the G-3 Advisor.

    b. <u>Maintenance.</u> The Vietnamese Marine Corps is authorized 1st through 3rd echelon maintenance for all communications-electronics equipment. Separated battalions are authorized 2nd echelon maintenance. All 3rd echelon maintenance is provided by the Maintenance Section, Division Communication Company. Fourth echelon and depot maintenance is provided through the 63rd Signal Battalion, ARVN. Close coordination with the 63rd Signal Battalion advisors is advised to ensure Vietnamese Marine Corps delivery of inoperable equipment for repair.

    c. <u>Radio Nets.</u> Vietnamese Marine Corps radio nets closely parallel those of the U. S. Marine Corps. The standardization of radio nets and their names is an area that requires constant attention. The VNMC relies heavily on CW for their long-range communications. The AN/GRC-106 radio sets have provided the long-range voice communication capability.

    d. <u>TO&E Review.</u> TO&E reviews are a continuing requirement due to the availability of new items of equipment and modernization program. The Communications Advisor reviews the signal items portion of all VNMC TO&Es, he must also review those items of motor transport, engineer and quartermaster that are considered communications-electronics. All recommended changes, additions or deletion should be coordinated with the Division CEO and the G-4 Advisor to ensure the necessary programming is accomplished. All items recommended should be contained in the MASF inventory listing to ensure ARVN supportability.

CHAPTER VII
PART V: ENGINEER

7500 <u>GENERAL</u>

1. The Vietnamese Marine Corps organization provides for an Engineer Battalion which consists of a Headquarters and Service Company; a Construction Company and three Combat Engineer Companies. Total Battalion strength is 30 officers and 375 enlisted personnel.

2. Typical engineer work involves combat operation, road construction and maintenance and vertical construction projects. The engineer battalion operates under staff cognizance of the Assistant Chief of Staff G-4, Vietnamese Marine Corps who is assisted by a Division Engineer Officer.

3. The Engineer Advisor, besides being the advisor to the Engineer Battalion and the Division Engineer, must also maintain a relationship with other units, i.e., NAVFORV, OICC, RMK, and ROICC. The Advisor must supervise/monitor USMCON programs, draw and issue material from RMK and NSA, maintain a working relationship with OICC/ROICC, maintain an adequate map supply for the MAU, and maintain the MAU office spaces.

7501 <u>VNMC ENGINEER BATTALION</u>

1. The primary duty of the Engineer Advisor is to assist, supervise, and aid the VNMV engineer components as the need arises. The primary duties may involve one or more of the following:

   a. Giving technical advice on engineering problems to include equipment maintenance.

   b. To supervise the USMCON construction program.

   c. To escort VNMC trucks through U.S. installations as required.

   d. To assist in development of necessary buildings and facilities through JGS.

   e. To monitor the Vietnamese dependent housing program and to coordinate that portion of the U.S. Navy dependent housing program that supports the Vietnamese Marine Corps.

   f. To oversee projects either an Advisor or Vietnamese Marine Corps initiated in order to best utilize existing assets.

2. To accomplish the above tasks successfully the Advisor will:

   a. Maintain a close relationship with the Division Engineer and the Engineer Battalion Commander. This relationship will normally be daily contact.

b. Ensure that U.S. provided assets are correctly utilized.

c. Provide U.S. personnel escort when necessary to transit or enter a U.S. facility.

d. Encourage and endorse projects to be accomplished through Vietnamese Marine Corps channels.

e. Maintain a file on dependent housing within the Vietnamese Marine Corps to indicate number of units on hand and the number required to house remaining dependents.

f. Maintain a close contact with Force Civil Engineer, NAVFORV, in order to have current knowledge of construction, road, and/or building status.

h. Screen excess listings for construction materials to aid the USMCON program.

7502 FORCE CIVIL ENGINEER, NAVFORV

1. This department monitors, approves, and provides the funds to support the USMCON and dependent housing project. It is a vital necessity that this office is constantly up-to-date on project status and requests for additional funds. The Engineer Advisor will:

a. Maintain close contact, at least once per week, and more often if necessary,

b. Submit requests for base camps as need arises through USMCON. Requests must specify unit strength, number/type vehicles, type of buildings desired. With this information, a design can then be formulated with total cost.

c. Submit requests to Force Civil Engineers for additional money to complete existing USCON projects. This request should include list of materials needed. NAVFORV will forward the material requirement to OICC, Plans and Programs, when money has been allocated.

d. Submit USMCOM program for Vietnamese Marine Corps to Force Civil Engineer when requested. This request is a yearly requirement.

e. Fulfill further requests from NAVFORV as they occur.

7503 RECEIPT/ISSUE OF U.S. FURNISHED MATERIALS

1. A majority of construction materials in support of USMCON are U.S. furnished materials. To ensure proper utilization of these materials the Advisor must first submit material requirements through Force Civil Engineer to OICC. OICC then purchases the material, normally from RMK. When notified by RMK that materials needed are ready for pick up, the Advisor must:

a. Determine number/type of transportation required.

    b. Escort the trucks into RMK Island Depot.

    c. Supervise loading of the trucks.

    d. Ensure all loads are secured.

    e. Receipt for all materials at the Shipping and Receiving Building.

    f. Issue to each driver the blue receipt so that each vehicle may leave the compound.

    g. Ensure that drivers do not pick up unauthorized gear/equipment.

    h. Escort the trucks and materials to job site and ensure materials are secured in building or have physical security.

    i. Monitor construction and ensure materials are used properly.

7504   OICC--PLANS AND PROGRAMS

1. This office is not directly in the chain-of-command. Normally requests are forwarded from Force Civil Engineer to OICC. The Engineer Advisor should visit this department to ensure that the necessary paper work has arrived to answer and vice-versa.

7505   ROICC--RESIDENT OFFICER-IN-CHARGE CONSTRUCTION

1. On each USMCON supported project, OICC provides a ROICC with staff. This department insures that the individual contractor is doing the work according to design and specifications. This contact is as frequent as necessary, a working relationship.

7506   MAP SUPPLY FOR MAU ADVISORS

1. The Engineer Advisor is responsible to maintain a map supply of the country of RVN. To maintain this supply, the advisor will:

    a. Ensure an inventory of maps is held frequently.

    b. Requisition maps as required from U.S. Naval Oceanographic Office, Saigon.

7507   MAU BUILDING MAINTENANCE

1. The Engineer Advisor has been assigned additional duty as maintenance officer. As necessary, the advisor will notify the Post Engineer of the building discrepancy. Normally a telephone call to the trouble desk will suffice. If a job is to consist of considerable work, a Post Engineer work request must be submitted.

7508 MASF PROGRAM

1. All major engineer items are processed through the MASF program. The Engineer Advisor will:

    a. Review TO&E to ensure that all equipment is not obsolete, ensure that the right type of equipment is programmed and proper distribution throughout the VNMC Division is made.

    b. Maintain an inventory list on each unit indicating the TO&E requirement for a particular item and showing actual O/H quantity.

    c. All changes, recommendation, and/or discrepancies are then reported to the G-4 Advisor.

CHAPTER VII
PART VI: SPECIAL SERVICES

7600 GENERAL

1. This directive is applicable to the Marine Advisory Unit. It is intended to set forth instructions to be used in connection with the duties of the Special Services Officer.

2. An Advisor will be appointed an additional duty as the Special Services Officer by the Senior Marine Advisor.

7601 SPECIAL SERVICES SUPPORT

1. The Marine Advisory Unit is supported by COMNAVFORV; specifically the Naval Support Activity, Saigon.

7602 REQUISITIONING OF SPECIAL SERVICES EQUIPMENT

1. All items of equipment must be requisitioned from Naval Support Activity, Saigon. Requisitions may be submitted on an as required basis.

7603 INTERNAL SUPPLY PROCEDURES

1. The Special Services Officer will keep formal records on all items of equipment $25.00 or over and on any other items the Senior Marine Advisor requires.

2. Advisors receiving special services equipment will sign a certificate of receipt. Upon return of the equipment, the receipt will be destroyed.

7604 REPORTS

1. Strength report is due by the 5th of each month with the officers and enlisted strength as of the first day of that month.

TAB A -- MAINTENANCE CHECK LIST FOR RADIO SETS

1. Clean with a cloth or soft brush all jacks, receptacles and switches.

2. Inspect the case for cracks or punctures.

3. Inspect the latches on the battery case and check the rubber gasket that seals the battery case to the radio to ensure that it is water tight.

4. Check the handset for cracks.

5. Ensure that the plastic protective covers in the mouthpiece and earpiece are intact.

6. Inspect the rubber gasket on the push-to-talk switch for tears.

7. Inspect the handset and speaker cords for frays.

8. Clean all foreign matter from the whip antenna (AT-271A/PRC). Clean the ferrules of all grit and tarnish (Blitz cloth or a rubber pencil eraser is excellent for this). The cleaner all antenna connections the better the antenna will function.

9. If your radio has been submerged or exposed to extremely heavy or prolonged rain, take advantage of the sun. When possible, remove the unit from its case and let it dry for a couple of hours.

10. Show your radio operator how to accomplish the above and supervise him.

11. When utilizing the RC-292 antenna, do no leave it erected for a prolonged period of time as the antenna elements. Ground plane elements and the mast sections will freeze together. At least once a week take the antenna down and clean all elements.

TAB B -- CHARACTERISTICS OF COMMONLY USED RADIO SETS

CHARACTERISTICS OF RADIO SET, AN/PRC-25 (AN/PRC-77)

Frequency: 30-75.95 MC

Power Output: 2 - 3 watts

Emission: Voice

Modulation: FM

Range:	Miles	KM
Whip antenna to whip antenna	5	8
Long wire to whip	8	12
Long wire to long wire	17	27
RC-292 to whip	8	12
RC-292 to RC-292	10	16

Compatible with AN/PRC-10, AN/VRC-46 or any of the AN/VRC-12 series.

NOTE: The AN/PRC-77 is identical in characteristics as that of the AN/PRC-25 with the exception of the capability to mount a cryptographic to the AN/PRC-77.

TAB B -- CHARACTERISTICS OF COMMONLY USED RADIO SETS

CHARACTERISTICS OF RADIO SET, AN/VRC-46

Frequency: 30-75.95 MC

Power Output: 3 watts LO PWR
35 watts HI PWR

Emission: Voice

Modulation: FM

Range:	Miles	KM
Whip antenna to whip antenna	20	32
RC-292 to whip	25	40
RC-292 to RC-292	30	48
Long wire to whip	25	40
Long wire to long wire	35	56

Compatible with AN/PRC-10, AN/PRC-25, AN/PRC-77 and any of the AN/VRC-12 series radios.

TAB B -- CHARACTERISTICS OF COMMONLY USED RADIO SETS

CHARACTERISTICS OF RADIO SET, AN/GRC-106

Frequency: 2-29.999 MC

Power output: 200-400 watts low power

Emission: Voice/CW/FSK

Modulation: AM/SSB (USB)

Range:	Miles	KM
Whip antenna to whip antenna	50	80
Long wire-to-long wire	100-1,	500 miles

Compatible with AN/PRC-74, AN/MRC-83 and AN/PRC-47

CHARACTERISTICS OF RADIO SET, AN/PRC-74

Frequency: 2-11.999 MC

Power output: 15 watts

Emission: Voice/CW

Modulation: AM/SSB (USB)

Range:	Miles	KM
Whip antenna to whip antenna	25	40
Long-wire to long-wire	Several hundred miles	

Compatible with AN/GRC-106, AN/PRC-47 and AN/MRC-83 (TRC-75)

NOTE: The range listed for the various antenna combinations are the maximum range under optimum operating conditions.

TAB C -- RC-292 ANTENNA CONFIGURATIONS

The RC-292 Antenna is an elevated ground plane antenna designed for use with radio sets AN/PRC-25, AN/PRC-77 and the AN/VRC-46. The antenna is an Omni directional quarters wave whip antenna. The theory of the elevated ground plane antenna (30-300 MC) is as follows:

At the VHF level, propagated radio waves are highly susceptible to ground loss and prevent efficient radiation or reception. In order to offset the ground loss, the whip antenna portion is elevated (only the vertical element of the RC-292 is the antenna) and an artificial ground is placed beneath it (the antenna elements which point downward) to reflect the radio waves which are radiated toward the ground. The resultant effect is a radio wave traveling through free space with minimum ground loss. If the ground plane elements are erected according to the following chart, optimum performance will result:

OPERATING FREQUENCY	VERTICAL ELEMENT SECTIONS				GROUND PLANE SECTIONS			
AB 21	AB 22	AB 23	AB 24	AB 21	AB 22	AB 23	BA 42	
30-36.5 MC	1	1	1	1	2	1	1	1
36.5-54.4 MC	None	1	1	None	1	1	1	1
54-70.0	None	None	1	1	None	1	1	1

STANDING OPERATING PROCEDURES FOR MARINE ADVISORY UNIT

TAB D - **PHIẾU KIỂM SOÁT BẢO TRÌ HÀNG TUẦN**
Weekly preventive maintenance check list

HỌ VÀ TÊN (TÀI XẾ): _____ NGÀY: _____
Driver's name   Date

QUÂN XA SỐ: _____ SỐ DẶM ANH: _____
Vehicle number   Mileage

TÊN CỦA CỐ VẤN: _____
Advisor's name

Cước chú (remarks)

1. Hằng tuần, Tài xế nên kiểm soát quân xa và dùng mẫu này để xin tu bổ hoặc sửa chữa. Các vật liệu sửa chữa ngoài khả năng của mình, chuyển tiếp đến chuyên viên bảo trì của đơn vị.
2. Chữ V (được) - X(Sửa chữa/thay thế) - O (xin điều chỉnh lại). Sau khi kiểm soát và ghi chú, chuyển phiếu này cho Cố Vấn.

1. Drivers will inspect vehicle weekly using this form. Adjust/repair as needed. Items beyond the driver's capability of repair are to be performed by unit maintenance personnel.
2. Letter V (OK) - X(repair/replace) - O(adjust). After checking these forms submit to the Advisor.

Loại I: **Động cơ** (Engine compartment)

1. DÂY LƯNG : _____   9. TAY LÁI (CHẶT CHẾ) : _____
   Belt   Steering (tightness)

2. BÌNH LỌC GIÓ : _____ 10. BÌNH LỌC NHỚT : _____
   Air cleaner   Oil filter

3. BÌNH GIẢM NHIỆT : _____ 11. BAO CÂY NHÚN : _____
   Radiator   Rocker arm cover

4. MỨC NHỚT : _____   12. SỰ SẠCH SẼ : _____
   Oil level   Cleanliness

5. BỘ LY KẾT : _____   13. BÌNH ĐIỆN : _____
   Linkages   Battery

6. SỰ LẮP ĐƯỜNG DÂY ĐIỆN: _____   a- CỰC ẮC QUI : _____
   Wiring   Cells

STANDING OPERATING PROCEDURES FOR MARINE ADVISORY UNIT

7. MÁY PHÁT ĐIỆN : _____   b- DÂY CÁP : _____
   Generator   Cables

8. MÁY PHÁT HÀNH : _____   c- SỰ SẠCH SẼ : _____
   Starter   Cleanliness

Loại II: Chảy - hở (Leaks)

1. NHỚT (ĐẦU MÁY) : _____   5. HỘP SỐ CHÍNH và PHỤ : _____
   Oil (Engine)   Transmission & Transfer case

2. NHỚT THẮNG : _____
   Brake fluid

3. BỘ PHẬN THẮNG BÁNH XE : _____   6. BỘ PHẬN TỐC : _____
   Wheel seals   Differential

4. BÌNH NƯỚC : _____   7. HỆ THỐNG THOÁT : _____
   Water   Exhaust system

Loại III: Tình trạng tổng quát - (General conditions)

1. SỰ SẠCH SẼ : _____   8. THẮNG TAY : _____
   Cleanliness   Hand brake

2. GHẾ : _____   9. ĐÈN : trước, sau, thắng, hiệu
   Seat   Lights: head, tail, brakes, direct
                                          ___/___/___/___

3. KIẾNG CHẮN GIÓ : _____
   Glass

4. BÀN ĐẠP (khoảng 1 phần Anh khi ở thế tự nhiên) : _____
   Clutch pedal (1" free play, approx.)

5. BÀN THẮNG (khoảng 1/2" phần Anh khi ở thế tự nhiên) : _____
   Brake pedal (½" play, approx.)

6. BẢNG ĐỒNG HỒ : _____   10. KIẾNG CHIẾU HẬU : _____
   Instrument panel   Mirrors

   a- ĐỒNG HỒ XĂNG : _____   11. THANH CẢN : _____
      Fuel guage   Bumpers

   b- ĐỒNG HỒ NHIỆT : _____   12. GIÁ NÂNG : _____
      Temp. guage   Lifting fixtures

STANDING OPERATING PROCEDURES FOR MARINE ADVISORY UNIT

    c- ĐỒNG HỒ ĐIỆN ĐẦU MÁY
       Battery/Gen. guage or light

    d- ĐỒNG HỒ ĐO ÁP LỰC NHỚT
       Oil pres. guage or light

    e- ĐỒNG HỒ VẬN TỐC
       Speedometer

    f- CÂY GẠT NƯỚC
       Windshield wipers

    g- CÒI XE
       Horn

7. Ổ KHÓA/DÂY XÍCH:
   Locks/Chain

13. ĐAI ỐC BÙ-LONG:
    Nuts & bolts (tightness)

14. HỆ THỐNG NHÚN
    Suspension system

    a- LÒ XO
       Spring

    b- HỆ GIẢM CHẤN
       Shock absorbers

    c- SƯỜN
       Chassis

Loại IV: Công-xuất - (power train)

1. MỨC NHỚT : _____
   Transmission oil level

2. CẦN SANG SỐ : _____
   Shift control

3. TOÀN BỘ : _____
   Assembly mount

4. TRỤC SƠ CẤP : _____
   Drive shafts

Loại V: Bánh xe - (tires)

1. ÁP LỰC HƠI VÀ ĐẦU VAN : _____
   Air pres. and valve caps

2. TAI ỐC VÀ ĐINH CHÌM : _____
   Lug nuts, retainer studs

3. VÀNH BÁNH : _____
   Rims

4. SỰ HAO MÒN VÀ NỨT : _____
   Wear and cuts

TAB E -- MAINTENANCE POINTS - 1/4-TON TRUCK AND M-606

1. As in maintenance of other items of equipment, the degree of care afforded the 1/4-ton truck will determine the length of trouble free service provided.

2. The following checkpoints and deficiencies, while second nature to most operators, are provided to emphasize their importance associated with user/operator maintenance (NOTE: Items underlined should be repaired immediately).

   a. Front

   (1) hood - safety catch <u>missing</u>, bent, not aligned, <u>broken</u>; hold down catches stuck, <u>broken</u>, <u>missing</u>.

   (2) cowl vent - jammed; screen clogged, broken, rusty, stuck.

   (3) turn signal lights - base loose; lens cracked; wires loose, frayed, <u>exposed</u>.

   (4) fenders - rusted, bent, cracked, crushed.

   (5) bumpers - U-channel bent, cracked, loose.

   (6) lifting shackles - stuck, bent, loose, missing; safety pin or chain missing.

   (7) windshield wipers - blades <u>broken</u>, <u>missing</u>; rubber cracked, cut, hardened.

   (8) headlights, blackout markers - <u>painted over</u>, dirty, <u>broken</u>; marker twisted out of line; blackout support bracket or shield loose, <u>broken</u>; <u>lenses waterlogged</u>, clogged.

   (9) windshield - <u>cracked enough to obstruct drivers vision</u>, crazed, discolored; weather-stripping cracked, torn, missing; glass broken; hood bumpers missing; glass broken.

   b. Rear

   (1) canvas, windows - torn, dirty; retaining straps frayed; buckled missing; seams open; windows fogged.

   (2) trailer coupling receptacle - damaged, corroded, screw, cover, or cover spring loose, missing; gasket missing.

   (3) reflector - painted over, <u>broken</u>, <u>missing</u>, not on spare wheel assembly.

   (4) towing pintle - not lubricated, rusted; spring broken, won't work.

(5) lifting shackles - bent, loose, stuck, rusty, <u>missing</u>; safety pin or chain broken, missing.

(6) bumperettes - bent, rusty, broken; bolts loose, <u>missing</u>.

(7) turn signals, lights - glass broken, dirty, <u>painted over</u>, <u>waterlogged</u>; wires frayed, <u>exposed</u>; loose.

(8) end panel - rusty, badly dented, seam cracks visible.

(9) spare wheel and tire - loose on mount, <u>flat</u>, <u>sidewalls cut</u>, tread worn off, wheel bent.

c. <u>Sides</u>

(1) tires and wheels - lug nuts <u>loose</u>, <u>missing</u>; studs bent, stripped; rims dented, bent; tire bead not snug on rim; wrong pressure; tires mismatched, <u>cut or worn to fabric</u>, unevenly worn.

(2) fuel tank - filler cap rusted, <u>missing</u>; gasket broken, missing vent valve in wrong position; tank leaking; strainer clogged, missing, unserviceable.

(3) side panels - bent, seams cracked, strap eyes crushed, missing; bow rod hold-downs bent, broken.

(4) mirror - <u>broken</u>, clouded, missing; bracket not adjustable.

d. <u>Inside</u>

(1) tool box - tools <u>broken</u>, <u>missing</u>; cover bent, crushed, <u>missing</u>.

(2) battery box - cover bent, clips loose or broken, box dirty, <u>corroded</u>.

(3) batteries - cracked, leaking, dirty; <u>clamps of post loose, corroded; electrolyte level low; low charge</u>; filler caps <u>loose</u>, broken, missing vents <u>clogged</u>; hold downs too tight, <u>loose, corroded</u>.

(4) seats - covers torn, frames bent, retaining pins or chains missing; safety cut, retaining eye <u>loose or broken, catch broken</u>.

(5) gauges, indicators - glass broken, painted over, clouded; unreadable; pointer missing.

(6) floor - rusted, drains clogged.

(7) <u>windshield - lock pins stuck, missing chain broken</u>.

(8) windshield wipers - hose cracked, loose, leaking, scraping glass or frame, loose.

e. Under the Hood

(1) horn - loose, corroded, won't work, connections loose.

(2) distributor - cracked, screws or lock washers missing; cables loose, seal missing.

(3) generator regulator - mount loose, connections loose, wires exposed.

(4) generator - out of line, loose pulley cracked, connector loose.

(5) linkage - badly worn, binding, bent, pins missing.

(6) oil filter cap - missing, gasket loose.

(7) radiator - cap missing, wrong; insulator cracked; tubes and hoses leaking, hard, cut; clamps loose, fins crushed or clogged; loose on mount.

(8) air cleaner - oil level low; grit in bowl; intake screen missing; leaking.

(9) intake manifold - bolts loose, gasket leaking, cracked.

(10) exhaust manifold - bolts loose, missing; gasket loose, missing.

(11) vacuum pump - loose, leaking.

(12) fan belt - too tight, loose, frayed, and cracked.

(13) master cylinder - vent hole clogged, cap too tight, loose; fluid low.

(14) oil dip stick - bent; O-ring cut or missing, won't seat right, missing; oil level low, below ADD.

(15) oil filter - loose, leaking.

(16) fuel lines - crushed, leaking.

f. Underneath

(1) drive shafts - U-joints - rattling, unlubed.

(2) rear differential -breather plugged, missing; suspension bolts loose, out of alignment; leaking.

(3) service brake lines - <u>leaking</u>, crushed; parking brake - loose, leaking bent, <u>oil drip fouling brake band</u>.

(4) transmission - transfer - <u>leaking</u>, breather cap stopped up, missing.

(5) flywheel- clutch housing - seals <u>leaking</u>.

(6) shock absorbers - bent, crushed, loose, broken.

(7) coil springs - <u>broken</u>, lopsided, gasket leaking; bolts loose, missing.

(8) oil pan - drain plug <u>loose</u>, leaking; gaskets leaking; bolts loose, missing.

(9) radiator drain cock - clogged, broken.

(10) differential - <u>dripping</u>; breather plugged or <u>missing</u>.

(11) front universals - nuts or bolts <u>loose</u>, <u>missing</u>, <u>rattling</u>, <u>poorly lubed</u>.

(12) front suspension - bolts loose, arms or cross-members <u>bent</u>, <u>missing</u>.

(13) steering - <u>loose</u>, nuts missing, grease fittings broken, missing.

(14) exhaust system - burn <u>holes</u> in <u>pipe</u>.

(15) suspension brackets - broken, missing, muffler leaking, crushed, rusted out.

g. <u>Operating Check</u>

(1) parking brake - boot torn, missing; <u>won't hold</u> on slope, won't engage and release smoothly.

(2) Ignition switch - lock nuts-screws loose, <u>missing</u> switch broken.

(3) warning lights - broken, painted over.

(4) wiper motors – <u>won't work</u>, weak, chatter.

(5) transfer - hard to operate, <u>won't engage</u> or <u>disengage</u> without stopping or clutching.

(6) clutch - grabs, chatters, slips; wrong free play.

(7) transmission - gearshift rattles, <u>sticks</u>, <u>loose</u>, <u>won't stay engaged</u> without excess noise or jumping out of gear.

(8) starter pedal - loose, works hard, <u>broken</u>, <u>won't work</u>.

(9) choke control and throttle control – sticking handles loose, missing.

* (10) battery - generator indicator - needle fails to register properly (high yellow or low green) while idling, <u>doesn't stay in green</u> while running.

* (11) oil pressure gauge - <u>fails to read 15-30 PSI when idling and close to 40 PSI at normal speeds</u>.

(12) accelerator pedal - <u>binds, sticks; loose, broken</u>.

(13) steering - wheel gouged or cracked, core rusted through; steering column loose, front end <u>shimmies</u> or <u>bounces, steers hard or loose</u>.

(14) headlights, blackout lights, turn signals – <u>won't light</u>, broken, operate improperly.

(15) speedometer - sticks, works erratically, <u>broken</u>.

(16) engine temperature gauge - fails to read 160 degrees to 180 degrees warmed up, around 200 degrees in usual operating conditions.

(17) service brakes - <u>spongy, wrong adjustment</u>.

3. As with other items of equipment, maintenance beyond the operator level must be performed by the supporting maintenance unit. Do not attempt repairs beyond the operator level.

* Does not apply to M-606

CHAPTER VIII
PART I: MEDICAL ADMINISTRATION

| PART I | MEDICAL | PARAGRAPH |

PROCESSING NEW ARRIVALS 8100

MEDICAL RECORDS AND RE-IMMUNIZATION 8101

SICK CALL 8102

PART II SANITATION

GENERAL 8200

PROGRAM 8201

IMPROVEMENT OF SANITATION PRACTICES 8202

PART III REPORTS

ADMINISTRATIVE REPORTS 8300

CHAPTER VIII
PART I: MEDICAL

8100 PROCESSING NEW ARRIVALS

1. Upon reporting for duty at the Marine Advisory Unit, field advisors will be issued a packet of various medical and prophylactic supplies consisting of:

    a. Anti-malaria tablets.

    b. Anti-diarrhea tablets.

    c. Salt tablets.

    d. One-a-day multiple vitamins.

    e. Water purification tablets.

8101 MEDICAL RECORDS AND RE-IMMUNIZATION

1. The Medical records of all Marine Advisory Unit personnel are maintained by the Medical Section and screened periodically to determine re-immunization requirements. Re-immunization is administered at the Marine Advisory Unit. The following schedules are provided and used as a guide for re-immunization:

    a. Gamma Globulin - upon entry in-country, 4 months later,

    b. Cholera - every 6 months.

    c. Plaque - every 6 months.

    d. Smallpox - every three years.

    e. Typhoid - every 3 years.

    f. Tetanus - every 6 months.

    g. Yellow fever - every 10 years.

    h. Influenza - yearly.

2. Yellow fever immunizations are given only at the 218th General Dispensary, Saigon on the first and third Tuesdays of each month between 1400 and 1500.

NOTE: Malaria discipline is most important. You must take one chloroquine/primaquine each week.

3. In the event personnel will not be in the Saigon area when reimmunizations are due, it is recommended that they stop at the nearest U.S. facility. Yellow fever immunizations are given only at special locations in Saigon and only twice each month. Special arrangements must be made to obtain the yellow fever immunization.

8102   SICK CALL

1. The Medical Section renders routine, mirror sick-call support to unit personnel. This service is quite limited because adequate treatment facilities are not available.

2. Definitive medical support is provided the Marine Advisory Unit by 218th General Dispensary on Tran Hung Dao Street, four blocks beyond the Plaza BEQ.

3. The 36th Medical Detachment provides dental support. This unit is physically located on the MACV Compound. Dental support is also provided by NAVFORV Dental Department.

4. The health or dental record, as appropriate, must accompany the Marine who seeks clinical support.

CHAPTER VIII
PART II: SANITATION

8200   GENERAL

1. The Medical Section expends much time and effort trying to elevate sanitation practices within the Vietnamese Marine Corps. Base Camps and dependent housing sanitation practices receive the most attention. A second major effort concerns vector, insect and rodent control measures both, in the field and in base camps.

8201   PROGRAM

1. The purpose consists of inspections, suggestions, recommendations and follow-ups.

8202   IMPROVEMENT OF SANITATION PRACTICES

1. Every advisor must constantly be alert for opportunities to impress upon his counterpart the need to improve sanitation practices.

CHAPTER VIII
PART III: REPORTS

8300 ADMINISTRATIVE REPORTS

1. The following reports are required:

    a. Patient Census Report at Vietnamese Marine Corps hospital must be given to G-3 every Friday morning.

    b. Each month a written report is given to MACV concerning all phases of the Vietnamese Marine Corps medical service.

CHAPTER IX
BRIGADE ADVISORY ELEMENT

PART I   **GENERAL**   **PARAGRAPH**

ADMINISTRATIVE REQUIREMENTS 9100

REPORTING 9101

CHAPTER IX
PART I: GENERAL

9100 <u>ADMINISTRATIVE REQUIREMENTS</u>

1. This chapter deals primarily with the administrative requirements of the Brigade Advisory Element which includes the Infantry Battalion Advisors.

2. Amplifying information is contained in other chapters of this SOP, Senior Marine Advisor directives, and MACV/NAVFORV Directives. TAB A is a pre-operation coordination check list for both Brigade and Battalion Advisors.

9101 <u>REPORTING</u>

1. SPOTREPs are submitted on an "as required" basis to the Control/OPCON Headquarters. The format for the SPOTREP varies with the Control Headquarters.

2. SITREPs are submitted by the Brigade Advisor on a daily basis to the G-3/Operations Advisor. The SITREP is called in, i.e., SSB, land line, teletype, using the format published in current Marine Advisory Unit Orders for Advisors. The Senior Brigade Advisor requires continuous input from Battalion Advisor to the Senior Marine Advisors and the OPCON Headquarters.

3. Reports of Serious Crime or Incidents are made immediately by the Senior Brigade Advisor to the Senior Marine Advisor and the OPCON Headquarters.

4. System for Evaluating the Effectiveness of ARVN (SEER).

    a. AMFES (Army and Marine Forces Evaluation System) is a subsystem of SEER and places two reporting requirements on the Marine Advisory Unit.

    (1) Quarterly Effectiveness Report is submitted in questionnaire and narrative form by the Infantry Battalion Advisor to the Senior Brigade Advisor. Pertinent questions are answered at each level and submitted to the G-3 Advisor of the Marine Advisory Unit not later than 30th day of the month of the calendar quarter under consideration: (e.g., by 30 December for the calendar quarter October - December).

    b. The report is submitted by the Marine Advisory Unit to MACV indicating the combat effectiveness of the Vietnamese Marine Corps.

5. After Action Reports if appropriate are prepared by the Senior Brigade Advisor after each action and submitted to MACV via the Senior Marine Advisor. Input is provided by the Battalion Advisors and incorporated into the Brigade report. Particular emphasis is placed on "Advisor Analysis" and "Recommendations".

TAB A -- RECOMMENDED PRE-OPERATIONS CHECKLIST

1. Situation

    a. Enemy - Designation, size location, weapons, and tactics employed by enemy forces in and adjacent to the operational area.

    b. Friendly Forces - Designation, location, size, weapons, mission, and capabilities of all available to include:

    (1) Artillery

    (2) Air (Fixed-Wing), Helicopter gunships

    (3) Boats (RAD or RAIDs)

    (4) Combat assault companies (VNN or US)

    (5) MEDEVAC

    (6) Naval Gunfire

    c. Adjacent Units - Designation, location, size, weapons, and mission of all adjacent units down to the lowest possible level, (e.g., Bn, Regt, Div).

2. Mission - Clearly defined statement of unit's mission.

3. Execution

    a. Concept of the operation at control headquarters level.

    b. Sequence of events to include DTG the OPCON is effected.

    c. Coordinating instructions, i.e., H-hour, D-day, and time supporting assets are on station.

4. Administrative and Logistics

    a. Deadline for normal support requests (e.g., request for C&C helicopter by 1800 on the proceeding day).

    b. Reports required by control headquarters, format, and time/method of submission (e.g., night positions by 1900, etc.).

c. Procedure for requesting and clearing (ground and political clearance) artillery, air, and naval gunfire.

d. Medevac format and special instructions (e.g., counterpart must parallel, U.S. Advisor must be in the PZ, what criteria is used for medevac priorities).

e. Frequency/telephone number of Marine Advisory Unit and reporting requirements (Times of SITREP reporting, and format).

f. Coordinate mail delivery and means of resupply for advisors.

g. All necessary maps, overlays (Picto and map supplements), to include the AO and sufficient boundaries.

5. Command and Communications

a. Determine the command arrangement at the Central HQ/TOC to insure that any requests or orders which require decision by your counterpart are paralleled by the Vietnamese commander having OPCON of the Vietnamese Marine Corps Brigade/Battalion.

b. Draw the necessary KACs or establish thrust point for radio security.

(1) Ensure that the Control Headquarters is aware of the amount of SOI, KACs required monthly.

(2) Check on the method of encoding and decoding used by the Control HQ/TOC.

c. Draw SOI and know the frequencies and call signs of all units listed in paragraph 1 B&C.

CHAPTER X
ARTILLERY ADVISORY ELEMENT

| PART I | GENERAL | PARAGRAPH |

ORGANIZATION 10100

PART II   REPORTS

SPOTREPs 10200

SITREPs 10201

SYSTEMS FOR EVALUATING THE EFFECTIVENESS OF
ARVN (SEER) 10202

PART III   ADMINISTRATION

TURN-OVER FILES 10300

CHAPTER X
PART I: GENERAL

10100 ORGANIZATION

1. Organization of the Vietnamese Division Artillery is as follow:

2. The Artillery Advisory Element is organized along the lines of the Vietnamese Marines' Division Artillery. In the Vietnamese Marine Corps, the Division Artillery Section is made up of 10 officers and 39 enlisted personnel and three artillery battalions, each one consisting of 48 officers and 453 enlisted personnel. The overall total of personnel for the Division Artillery is 154 officers and 1,398 enlisted Vietnamese Marines.

3. The Artillery Advisor provides advice in artillery fire direction, tactical fire direction, fire support coordination, battery gunnery procedures and artillery material (provides assistance and advice on maintenance of weapons, vehicles and other equipment). In addition, the artillery advisor has other duties, which are not directly related to his specialty. These duties include: heliborne techniques both day and night, personnel welfare, morale, pay, promotions, decorations, leave, liberty and any other aspect of the system that could affect the units performance of duty.

4. The employment of artillery normally is one artillery battalion in direct support of one Vietnamese Marine Brigade. Situations do arise when artillery batteries are deployed individually, under the operational control of other than Vietnamese Marine units.

CHAPTER X
PART II: REPORTS

10200 <u>SPOTREPs</u>

1. SPOTREPs are submitted on an "as required" basis to the Central/OPCON Headquarters. The format for the SPOTREP varies with the Central Headquarters.

10201 <u>SITREPs</u>

1. When operating as a separate artillery battalion or battery, not under the OPCON of Vietnamese Marine Corps units, the Artillery Advisory will, if direct communication means is available, report to the G-3 Advisor, Marine Advisory Unit on a daily basis. When direct communications means is not available, the Artillery Advisor will request that his SITREP be forwarded to the G-3 Advisor, Marine Advisory Unit by his higher headquarters. The SITREP will follow the published format in current Marine Advisory Unit orders for advisors.

10202 SYSTEM FOR EVALUATING THE EFFECTIVENESS OF ARVN (SEER) (See Marine Advisory Unit Order 3000.1)

CHAPTER X
PART III - ADMINISTRATION

10300   <u>TURN-OVER FILES</u>

1. The Division Artillery Advisor and all Senior Artillery Battalion Advisors will maintain in their possession current Turn-over Files. These files will be consistent with the current Marine Advisory Unit order for advisors concerning Turn-over Files.

CHAPTER XI
FIELD DEPLOYMENT OF MARINE ADVISORY UNIT

| PART I | INTRODUCTION | PARAGRAPH |

GENERAL 11100

PART II   THE ADVANCE PARTY

COMPOSITION 11200

DUTIES AND RESPONSIBILITIES 11201

PART III   THE MAIN COMMAND POST

COMPOSITION 11300

ORGANIZATION 11301

PART IV   THE ADMINISTRATIVE COMMAND POST

COMPOSITION 11400

DUTIES AND RESPONSIBILITIES 11401

CHAPTER XI
PART I: INTRODUCTION

11100 <u>GENERAL</u>

1. In the event that the Vietnamese Marine (VNMC) deploys in division strength the Marine Advisory Unit (MAU) will deploy to support the VNMC Division. The MAU will be divider into two command posts. The offices in the Bo Tu Lenh will be designated as the administrative command post. That portion of the advisory unit which deploys with the Marine Division will be designated as the Main Command Post (MCP). The MCP will be co-located with the VNMC Division command post in the field. An advance party from the MCP will deploy with the first VNMC units in order to provide continuous support for the VNMC and to organize the command post for the arrival of the remainder of the personnel. (For details of deployment see TAB B--Movement Plan.)

CHAPTER XI
PART II: THE ADVANCE PARTY

11200 COMPOSITION

1. The Advance Party will be composed of the G-3 Advisor, G-1 Advisor, Assistant Engineer Advisor, Supply Advisor and one Vietnamese interpreter.

2. Additional personnel will be added to the Advance Party as circumstances warrant.

11201 DUTIES AND RESPONSIBILITIES

1. The Advance Party will deploy with the first units of the VNMC. They will establish initial coordination with the VNMC and all supporting units. They will establish the MAU MCP in preparation for the arrival of the remainder of the MAU. The Advance Party will be responsible for normal MAU advisory functions until the arrival of the remainder of the MAU staff.

2. The G-3 Advisor will establish liaison with the VNMC G-3 and serve as the point of contact between the Advance Party and the Vietnamese Marine Corps Division. In the absence of either the Senior Marine Advisor (SMA) or the Assistant Senior Marine Advisor (ASMA), the G-3 Advisor will command the Advance Party. In this capacity, he will represent the MAU until the MCP is established or he is relieved by proper authority.

3. The G-1 Advisor will perform the duties of Headquarters Commandant. He will be responsible for preparation of the camp for the arrival of the MCP personnel. Specific duties will include:

    a. Supervision of working party provided by VNMC.

    b. Establishment of billeting and messing facilities.

    c. Supervision of construction of latrines and sanitary facilities.

    d. Establishment of mail and guard mail system between the MCP and the administrative command post.

    e. Organizing and supervision of a system for mail distribution and internal routing.

4. The Assistant Engineer Advisor will be responsible for the following:

    a. Establishing liaison with U.S. engineering units in the area.

    b. Assisting the VNMC in procurement of construction and barrier materials.

c. Providing technical assistance to the G-1 Advisor in construction of CP facilities.

d. Coordinating with the VNMC to ensure adequate utilities support.

e. Monitoring the defensive minefield situation.

f. Ensuring an adequate supply of maps for use by the division advisory staff.

5. The Supply Advisor will be responsible for the following:

a. Establishing liaison with appropriate U.S. support facilities to ensure adequate logistics support for the MCP operations.

b. Assisting the VNMC in organization and operation of the helicopter pick-up zone until the MCP is functioning. (See TAB B--Pick-Up Zone Operations.)

CHAPTER XI
PART III: THE MAIN COMMAND POST

11300 <u>COMPOSITION</u>

1. In addition to the advance party, the MCP will be composed of the SMA, G-4 Advisor, Senior Medical Advisor, Senior Artillery Advisor, G-2 Advisor, Communications Advisor, Operations Chief, Supply Administrative Man, Communications Maintenance Advisor, Motor Transport Mechanical Advisor and designated administrative support personnel.

2. Additional personnel will be rotated between the administrative command post and the MCP as necessary.

11301 <u>ORGANIZATION</u>

1. The Main Command Post will be organized into three functional sections. These sections will be the Headquarters Section, the Logistics Section, and the Operations Section.

    a. The Headquarters Section will be headed by the G-1 Advisor who will be designated the Headquarters Commandant. The section will include the supply administrative man, Vietnamese interpreter, and administrative and housekeeping functions. These duties shall include routine administration, billeting, supervision of all assigned Vietnamese personnel, security, mail routing and distribution, operation of a mess, if feasible, and necessary facilities construction. The Headquarters Commandant will be assisted in the performance of these duties by members of other sections as necessary.

    b. The Logistics Section will be headed by the G-4 Advisor. The section will include the Medical Advisor, Supply Advisor, Assistant Engineer Advisor, Motor Transport Advisor, Motor Transport Mechanical Advisor, and Communications Maintenance Advisor. The section will be responsible for assisting the Vietnamese in all matters pertaining to the normal logistics functions. Additional responsibilities will include providing supply support for the advisory staff (See TAB A--List of Equipments) and assisting the Vietnamese in Logistics Support Area (LSA) operations in the helicopter Pick-up Zone (PZ). When tasked by the Headquarters Commandant the Logistics Section will assist in facilities construction.

    c. The Operations Section will be headed by the G-3 Advisor. The section will include the Division Artillery Advisor, G-2 Advisor, Training Advisor, Communications Advisor, Assistant Training Center Advisor and the Operations Chief. The section will be responsible for assisting the Vietnamese in operations planning and supporting arms coordination as required. In addition to the normal advisory function, the section will operate a Tactical Operations Center (TOC) on a 24-hour basis (See TAB E--FSCC/TOC Operations), establish liaison with all U.S. elements in the area, establish required radio nets and act as net control (See TAB C--Communications Plan).

2. Close coordination and cooperation between all sections is mandatory for the success of any operation. Any confusion over assigned responsibilities which cannot be resolved between the parties concerned will be referred to the SMA for early resolution.

CHAPTER XI
PART IV: THE ADMINISTRATIVE COMMAND POST

11400 COMPOSITION

1. The administrative command post will be composed of the ASMA, Administrative Officer, Assistant G-3 Advisor, Training Center Advisor, Song Than Advisor, Engineer Advisor, Medical Service Advisor, Ordnance Advisor, Logistics Chief, and designated administrative personnel.

2. Members of the administrative command post will be substituted for members of the MCP at the direction of the SMA.

11401 DUTIES AND RESPONSIBILITIES

1. The administrative command post will be responsible for the routine operations of the MAU in the Saigon area. In addition to normal functions the administrative command post will serve as the rear echelon for the MCP. Normal radio contact will be maintained (See TAB C) and semiweekly courier runs will be established. Where appropriate, the administrative command post will keep COMNAVFORV and COMUSMACV informed of the progress of the operations.

TAB A -- LIST OF EQUIPMENT

1. The following list of equipment is considered to be the minimum for continuous operation of the command post. Five days' initial rations are included. Personal gear carried is at the option of the individual advisor, but should be held to a minimum.

2. Responsibilities for acquiring, packing, and shipment are as follows:

    a. The Supply Officer will ensure that all listed equipment is available prior to deployment, and supervise the packing of material for shipment.

    b. The Supply Administrative man will coordinate with all sections and be responsible for packing of material for shipment.

    c. The Motor Transport Advisor will ensure that all packed material can be mobile loaded and provide transportation as required.

    d. All sections will provide personnel to assist in packing and loading materials under the supervision of the Supply Advisor.

3.

ITEM	QUANTITY
Maps	5 copies of appropriate sheets
Pencil, grease	1 box, assorted colors
Paper, bond	1 ream
Map board	1
Code sheets for period	
Ball point pen, black	1 box
Coleman lantern	2
Candles	1 dozen
GP tent (small)	1 (billeting of personnel)
Tent, arctic	1 (SMA)
Radio, AN/PRC-25	2
Radio, AN/PRC-77	4
Antenna, RC-292	4
Jeep	3
Cot	5
Rubber mattress	5
Blanket	5
Hammer	2
Nails (assorted sizes)	5 pounds
Meal Combat Individual	75 meals (7 cases)
Long-Range Patrol Rations	1 case
Flashlight	5
Masking tape	1 roll (2")

Contact paper	1 roll
Battery, BA-30	2 dozen
Battery, BA-4386	20 batteries (for 25, 77, KY-38)
Water cans	5
Handsaw	2

4. Equipment to be carried by main CP group:

Field safe	2
Field desk w/folding stools	4
Locks (for field desk and fuze box)	8
Tables, folding	4
Typewriter, short carriage	2
Pencil, lead	2 dozen
Pen, ink, blue	2 dozen
Pencil sharpener	2
Pencil, grease, assorted colors	2 dozens each
Tape, masking	10 rolls (2")
Tape, scotch	10 rolls (1")
Paper, bond	2 reams
Paper, carbon snap out	3 reams
Paper, flimsy	4 reams
Hole punch	1 (2-hole)
Hole punch	1 (3-hole)
Calendar, desk	4
Stapler	2
Staples, box	4
Thumb tacks	12 dozen
Map tacks, box, assorted colors	3 each
Folders, manila	3 dozen
Fasteners, Acco	3 dozen
Acetate, roll	2 (48-inch or 58-inch)
Eraser, typewriter	5
Envelope, 9" x 4"	3 dozen
Envelope, 9" x 11"	3 dozen
Envelope, 12" x 16"	3 dozen
Maps of operational area	
Fuze box with hasp	4
Map board	3
Code sheets for initial period	
FMFM 3-1 (Staff Manual)	1
FMFM 7-1 (Staff Manual)	1
FMFM 3-3 (Helicopter Operations)	1
FMFM 4-6 (Air Movements of Units)	1
Cup, paper	5 dozen

Coffee pot	2
Coleman lantern	10
Candles	4 dozen
Battery BA-30	2 box
Flashlight	24
Broom	4
Brush	4
Tent CP	2
Tent CP (Small)	1
Hammer	
Nails	8d, 5 lbs; 10d, 5 lbs; spike 20d, 20 lbs
Vacuum can for coffee	2
Jeep	7
Radio AN/PRC-77	5
Radio AN/PRC-25	2
Antenna, RC-292	4
AN/GRC-106 (Unmounted)	1
AN/VRC-46 (Unmounted)	1
KY-38 and KYK-28	10
AN/PRC-74B	4
AN/GRA-39B	2
Battery, BA-4386	Provided by VNMC Communication Battalion as needed
PP-1451 (Battery charger)	1
TE-33	2
TA-312/PT	8
MX-306/WD-1	1 roll
Cot	20 (1 per person)
Air mattress	20 (1 per person)
Meal, Combat Individual	20 cases
Inspect repellent	3 cases
Supply records and files	As required
Heat tablets	1 case
Water can	24
Gas can	12
Lister bag	2
Long-Range Patrol Rations	10 cases
SP Pack	2 cases
Mosquito net	25
Clothing (cold weather)	As required depending on operational area.

TAB B -- MOVEMENT PLAN

1. Organization for Movement

   a. <u>General</u>

   (1) The Marine Advisory Unit will be organized into two movement units, formed around the following major troop organizations:

   > VNMC Division Advance Party
   > VNMC Division Main Command Post

   (2) Substitutions for members and/or changes of members composing the two movement units will be directed separately by the Senior Marine Advisor.

   b. <u>Assignments</u>

   (1) VNMC Division Advance Party:

   > G-3 Advisor
   > G-1 Advisor
   > Assistant Engineer Advisor
   > Supply Advisor
   > Vietnamese interpreter

   (2) VNMC Division Main Command Post:

   > Senior Marine Advisor
   > G-4 Advisor
   > Senior Medical Advisor
   > Division Artillery Advisor
   > G-2 Advisor
   > Communications Advisor
   > Motor Transport Advisor
   > Motor Transport Mechanical Advisor
   > Assistant Training Center Advisor
   > Training Advisor
   > G-3 Operations Chief
   > Supply Administration Man
   > Communications Maintenance Advisor
   > Designated Administrative personnel

c. Movement

(1) Staff advisors are responsible for the assembly and loading of material organic to their respective sections in accordance with the published movement schedule. The Motor Transport Advisor will supervise cargo loading as necessary.

(2) The Supply Advisor is responsible for coordination and movement of the MAU general cargo in accordance with the published movement schedule.

(3) The movement schedule will be coordinated by the G-3 Advisor.

(4) Insofar as practicable, all supplies and equipment will be scheduled for movement to the embarkation areas (i.e., Tan Son Nhut Airfield, Golf Beach) to coincide with loading schedules.

(5) Bulk cargo will be combat loaded aboard two M-35A2 2 1/2-ton 6x6 cargo trucks provided by the Transportation Company, Vietnamese Marine Corps.

(6) The palletizing of supplies, if required, will be coordinated by the Supply Advisor and the Motor Transport Advisor.

3. Personnel

a. Uniform, Equipment, and Baggage. Published at the time of movement by separate directive.

b. General Instructions

(1) Working parties and security personnel will move to the embarkation point with the equipment/cargo.

(2) The Advance Party will move to the embarkation point as determined by the arrival of its transportation.

(3) The Supply Advisor will provide Class I supplies to both the Advance Party and MCP personnel during the movement phase.

c. Movement of the Main Command Post. The MCP will move to the embarkation point with the VNMC Division main command post.

4. Embarkation areas

a. Assignment of areas of embarkation points

(1) Published at time of movement by separate directive.

(2) Direct liaison is authorized between the MAU Motor Transport Advisor and the port authority at the embarkation point for coordination and implementation of the movement plan.

b. <u>Material Handling Equipment</u>. Requirements for materials handling equipment in excess of the embarkation point control capability will be determined by the Motor Transport Advisor, and provisions made by him to compensate for any shortfall.

c. <u>Security</u>. Upon execution of this movement plan, the G-4 Advisor will be responsible for security of MAU equipment/cargo within the assigned embarkation areas, consonant with port control/authority directives and procedures.

5. Embarkation Schedules

a. <u>Dates</u>. Published by separate directive.

b. <u>Embarkation Points</u>. Published by separate directive.

6. Control

a. <u>Traffic Circulation and Control</u>. The Motor Transport Advisor will be responsible for traffic circulation and control measures within assigned U.S. embarkation areas and will coordinate these measures with the respective U.S. port authorities.

b. <u>Embarkation Control</u>. The Motor Transport Advisor will act as the MAU liaison representative to the port authority/control. After departure of the Motor Transport Advisor the Motor Transport Mechanical Advisor will perform this function. The Motor Transport Mechanical Advisor will ride the last flight to the operational area.

7. Miscellaneous

a. <u>Loading Plans</u>

(1) Individual ship/aircraft load planning will be coordinated by the Motor Transport Advisor for all MAU assigned personnel, and MAU equipment/cargo.

(2) Load planning guidance for specific types of ships/aircraft will be provided prior to the movement phase, by the Motor Transport Advisor.

TAB C -- MAU COMMUNICATIONS IN A DIVISION DEPLOYMENT

1. Organization. The Communications Advisor and the Technical Advisor will both initially deploy with the Marine Advisory Unit MCP. After establishing liaison with the Senior Signal Agency in the area, communications will be established on a division level. Brigade communications needs and problems will be channeled through the Communications Advisor.

2. Advance Party Communications

    a. It is not anticipated that an Advance Party Communication Team will be sent out because one of the Vietnamese Marine Corps brigades will probably already be established in the area, with communications to adjacent and higher units, and to the Marine Advisory Unit rear at Saigon. The MAU CP group, upon arrival in the tactical area, will simply phase in its communication equipment and take over the brigade's role as far as lateral, higher and MAU rear communications are concerned.

    b. In the event that a brigade is not established in the target area, the Communications Advisor will make liaison with the Senior Signal Officer in the area and accompany the Advance Party, taking sufficient equipment with the MAU Advance Party to establish any required radio nets. The Technical Advisor will remain with the main group and bring up the remaining necessary equipment.

3. Codes

    a. All operations codes (AKAC/USKAC) Signal Operating Instructions (SOIs), Numeric Encryption Codes (CIRCE) and Secure Voice Key Lists (NESTOR) will be obtained by the Communications Advisor from the area Senior Signal Officer either before or immediately after arrival in the operational area. The Communications Advisor will assume the task of redistribution within the MAU. He will further ensure that all units with which the MAU CP may be dealing have access to common codes and key lists.

    b. Distribution of codes and key lists will be as follows:

	HQ	REAR	BDE 147	BDE 258	BDE 369
USKAC OPS CODE	4	1	11	11	11
ADAC NUMERICAL CODE (CIRCE)	6	1	12	12	12
AREA SOI	4	1	6	6	6
AKAC KEY LIST (NESTOR)	3	0	6	6	6
KAL 55B (CIRCLE WHEEL)	3	2	12	12	12
MAU SOI AND CODES	50	2	15	15	15

4. Equipment. The distribution of equipment on hand as of 20 July 1971 will be as follows, except that the brigade(s) co-located with the MAU CP may be required to furnish equipment to the MAU CP:

	HQ	REAR	TRNG CENT	BDE 147	BDE 258	BDE 369
AN/GRC-106 Stationary	1*	1	0	0	0	0
AN/GRC-106/VRC-46 Mounted in M151	0	0	0	1	1	1
AN/VRC-46 Stationary	1	1	0	0	0	0
RC-292 Antenna	3	1	1	6	6	6
AN/PRC-77	8	0	0	8	8	8
AN/PRC-25	1*	0	1*	9*	9*	9*
KY-38 and KYK-28	6	0	0	8	8	8
TA-312/PT	8*	0	0	0	0	0
AN/PRC-74B	1	0	0	1	1	1
PP-1451 Battery Charger	1*	1	0	0	0	0
PP-2953	0	0	1	0	0	0

Note:*not rated on MAU T/A—on temporary loan.

5. Radio Nets

   a. The following nets will be established by the Advance Party as required.

NET	USE	EQUIPMENT	SECURE VOICE
DivAdmin	AdminTrf w/Saigon	AN/GRC-106	No
DivAdv Cmd #1	Command/TAC	AN/PRC-77	Yes
DivAdv Cmd #2	Command/TAC	AN/PRC-77	Yes
DivAirLiaison0 #1	Helo C&l	AN/PRC-25	No
DivAirLiaison)#2	Helo Liaison	AN/PRC-77	Yes
DivArty CTL	Tactical	AN/PRC-77	Yes
DivAirborneCoord	Tactical	AN/PRC-25	No
Higher Hq AreaCmd	Tactical	AN/PRC-77	Yes

All the above nets will not be needed at first, but will be phased in as the tactical situation develops. The G-3 Advisor will direct the priority of net activation. Two FM radios will be needed for landing zone control. Helicopters will initially report to the TOC on the Division ALO Net #1 and if necessary then be switched over to either the Division Airborne Coordination Net or Division Command #2, depending on whether two separate frequencies are needed. Hot lines will be established from each LZ to the TOC to facilitate LZ officers and TOC communications. Due to the shortage of radios and RC-292s, it may be necessary for the brigades(s) located adjacent to the Division CP to give up some communication equipment as necessary to support the various liaison officers. No more than a total of three liaison officers are anticipated.

b. In the event an Advance Party is necessary, the Communications Advisor will be prepared to activated the following nets:

> Division Advisor Command #1—Secure voice
> Division Administration
> Area Command/Tactical—Secure voice

To activate the Division Administrative Net, the Communications Advisor will use one of the brigade's AN/GRC-106s mounted in an M151 until such time as the rear party arrives with the unmounted AN/GRC-106. Deployed brigades having traffic for the MAU rear will pass it through the MAU CP.

6. Call Signs. Calls are assigned to the brigades and to the MAU CP by the Senior Signal Officer (SSO) Advisor in the area in which MAU units operate. Calls are listed in Advisor Signal Operating Instructions (SOI) which are available for using units from the SSO.

7. Frequencies. Primary and alternate frequencies are assigned to MAU units by the SSO in the area. Do not use the alternate frequency without prior permission from the SSO because it is likely some other unit's primary frequency. The Communications Advisor will deal with the SSO on any frequency problems.

8. Communications Security

   a. <u>NVA Intercept Capability</u>. In the spring of 1971, captured documents and personnel revealed the presence of over 4,000 NVA crypto-analysts in the SEA area. All were capable of copying English broadcasts, copying 120 characters per minute and decrypting 70 % to 80% of the traffic intercepted. The NVA is no longer using the AN/PRC-10 because they have obtained sufficient quantities of AN/PRC-25 radios.

   b. <u>KY-38 Secure Voice Equipment</u>. The use of secure voice equipment is strongly encouraged for any tactical communication. While the equipment is usually maintained in the clear mode, it is easily switched to the encrypter mode. This equipment should also be made easily available for the brigade commander and his battalion commanders to use, but they are not authorized custody. One important point to remember in order to avoid equipment breakdown, is to turn off the KY-38 and AN/PRC-77 prior to changing frequencies, keying with the KYK-28, or changing batteries.

   c. <u>Codes</u>. Use the codes and numeric encryption devices as much as possible in order to keep information from the enemy as long as possible. When using the OPCODES, the whole message <u>must</u> be encrypted, not just portions.

9. Maintenance

   a. <u>General</u>. The Communications and Technical Advisors are available for troubleshooting the radio equipment within the MAU. In the event of actual equipment breakdown, deliver it to the Communications Advisor who will "direct-exchange" the item, if

possible, and evacuate the faulty gear to the nearest U.S. Army repair facility as determined by the SSO in the area. Never turn in the AN/PRC-77 radio or any item of secure voice equipment to ARVN repair because only U.S. Army/U.S. Navy facilities have the necessary skills and parts.

    b. <u>RC-292 Antenna</u>. If neglected, the RC-292 antenna will become unserviceable due to rapid corrosion and "rusting shut" of the antenna elements. All elements should be installed with a light coating of clear grease or oil and screwed in finger tight and backed off one full turn. These elements should be checked, twisted and cleaned every two weeks.

10. Counterpart Relationships. Prior planning must be effected by the Communications Advisor with the Vietnamese Marine Corps Communications-Electronics Officer in order to avoid inadequate mutual support during the initial one or two hectic days of a division's deployment. The MAU will need the aid of Communications Battalion in the erection of RC-292 antennas and the laying of hot lines. The Communications Battalion is also tasked with providing batteries for MAU communication equipment. The VNMC will need early establishment of secure voice equipment to enable the Division Commander to talk with his brigade commanders. The MAU and VNMC CP must also strive to remote as many RC-292 antennas as possible away from the TOC in a dispersed manner.

TAB D -- PICK UP ZONE OPERATIONS

1. General. Due to the restrictions of road mobility encountered in most areas into which the Vietnamese Marine Division may be deployed, detailed considerations must be given to:

    a. Establishing helicopter pick-up/landing zones for troop movements, logistics operations and medical evacuation.

    b. Controlling of the pick-up/landing zones.

    c. Controlling of the helicopters in the pick-up/landing zones.

2. Responsibility

    a. All items mentioned in this tab are the ultimate responsibility of the Vietnamese Marine Corps, but are listed here to delineate responsibility for advice and assistance.

    b. Upon arrival of the Division CP in the field, the G-4 is responsible for the establishment of the LSA and helicopter pick-up zones. The G-4 Advisor will assist with establishing procedures for control of the zones, control of the helicopters working the zones, and organization of working parties in the zones.

    c. The Supply Advisor will be in the Division advance party and will be responsible for initiating the action required by paragraph 2.b. above.

    d. Although helicopter support teams are established by T/O, the advisor assigned to assist in the helicopter zones will ensure that the G-4 Advisor is kept informed of the adequacy of personnel working in the pick-up/landing zones to facilitate efficient operations.

3. Establishing Pick-up/Landing Zones

    a. Normally three helicopter support zones should be established for division field operations:

        (1) Troop and resupply zone.
        (2) Heavy lift zone.
        (3) Medical evacuation zone.

    b. The troop and resupply zone should be a fairly level area capable of receiving or dispatching four to six UH-1 helicopters simultaneously. It should be near enough to the CP to lend itself to observation and supervision, but at such a distance as not to disturb operations or living areas. The zone should be accessible by road for delivery of troops or light supplies. The zone should be organized so that all classes of supplies can be readily identified and located. Loading sites should be grouped according to destination of supplies.

c. The heavy-lift zone should be a fairly level area capable of receiving or dispatching at least two CH-47 or CH-54 helicopters simultaneously. The zone should be close enough to operation and living areas to ensure security, but should be so positioned as to avoid requiring loaded aircraft to fly over billeting and working areas. Approach and retirement lanes should not interfere with aircraft lanes for other zones. The zone must be accessible by road. Typical heavy loads are 105mm ammunition, light vehicles, 105mm Howitzers and bulldozers.

d. The medical evacuation zone should be fairly level and capable of receiving or dispatching two UH-1 helicopters simultaneously. The zone should be close to the site of the division hospital but not such as to cause dust and debris disturbed by rotor wash to contaminate the hospital area. The zone should be accessible to the hospital by road, but, for morale purposes far enough away from living and working areas to avoid transporting dead and seriously wounded through living and working areas.

e. Landing sites in each zone should be clearly marked and readily identifiable.

4. Control of the Zone

a. The G-4 Advisor, or his designated representative, will assist the Vietnamese in exercising positive control of the zone at all times and particularly during helicopter operations. It is desirable to have a U.S. advisor available to assist in controlling each zone.

b. Vehicular traffic should be confined to the periphery of the zones and then only to pick up or deliver troops and supplies. All other vehicles should be restricted from entering the zone area. No vehicle will be allowed in the zone during helicopter operations with the exception of ambulances for medical evacuation. An MP should be assigned to control vehicular traffic around the zone.

c. Foot traffic in the zone should be kept to a minimum at all times. During helicopter operations, only HST working party and supervisory personnel will be allowed in the zone with the exception of medical personnel for medical evacuation. When troops are to be transported, they should be kept well away from the landing sites until actually ready to board and quickly moved well away when landing in the zone. The Vietnamese G-4 should exercise continuous positive control over all Vietnamese personnel in the zone.

5. Control of Helicopters

a. The G-3 Advisor, through the ALO in the FSSC, will maintain positive control of all helicopter assets in the division.

b. The G-3 and G-4 Advisors will conduct liaison each evening, unless required more often and established a written priority listing for the next day's helicopter operations as necessary to support the division operations. The ALO will prepare a mission and sortie assignment table (see enclosure (1)). Should requirements change, the schedule may be changed only after coordination between the G-3 and G-4 Advisors.

c. The G-4 Advisor, or his designated representative, will be in the zone at all times while helicopters are operating in the zone to ensure aircraft personnel safety, proper aircraft utilization, and to counter any misunderstanding caused by language difference.

d. The G-4 Advisor, or his designated representative, will brief the mission commander or lead aircraft commander for each mission. The Vietnamese representative should be encouraged to conduct the brief. As a minimum the brief will contain the following information:

(1) Number and type of sorties.
Pick-up zone location.
Landing zone location.
Call sign and frequency of the controller in the pick-up and landing zones.
Weather in the pick-up and landing zones.
Enemy situation, time, and location of the last enemy contact.
Obstacles and hazards in the pick-up and landing zones.
Method of identifying the zones, i.e., smoke, air panel.
Fire support coordination arrangement, zone preparation, changes to normal procedures for announcing air warning, and data for artillery fires.

e. If possible, heavy-lift helicopters should be controlled on a frequency separate from other operational traffic due to the necessity of passing many more instructions to the aircraft by radio and overloading the net.

STANDING OPERATING PROCEDURES FOR MARINE ADVISORY UNIT

TAB E — FSCC/TOC OPERATIONS

1. Organization. The Vietnamese Marine Corps (VNMC) Division FSCC/TOC will consist of representatives from the G-1, G-2, G-3, G-4, FSCC, VNAF Tactical Air Party, and liaison personnel as necessary. The division operations and employment of supporting arms will normally be directed and monitored from the FSCC/TOC. The Fire Support Coordination Center and Tactical Operations Center will be co-located to provide immediate response of supporting arms to the tactical situation. The VNMC Division G-3 section will provide an Officer in Charge (OIC) and coordinator for the TOC. The Division Artillery Section will provide the Division Fire Support Coordinator and sufficient personnel to staff the FSCC. The Division Chief of Staff or VNMC G-3 will normally be located in or near the FSCC/TOC for timely decisions affecting operations of the division.

2. Advisory Support of the FSCC/TOC. Advisory support to the FSCC/TOC shall consist of paralleling VNMC requests for U.S. support, with advice on the best use of supporting arms, and assistance with the expeditious processing of operational requirements. The FSCC/TOC will operate under the staff cognizance of the G-3 Advisor. The advisory watch will normally be conducted on a 24-hour basis and organized as follows:

    a. The Division Artillery Advisor is designated as the Officer in Charge of the FSCC/TOC and will serve as the Senior Watch Officer. His duties will include:

    (1) Preparation of the watch schedule and coordination of efforts for sustained operation.
Supporting U.S. artillery and air liaison officers will operate under his supervision.

    (2) Advise and assist with preparation of the Division Fire Support Plan.

    (3) Consolidation of requests for helicopter (C&C, Air Cavalry, Admin, Logistic, etc.) support. In absence of a U.S. ALO, he will prepare and submit request for air assets to higher headquarters.

    (4) Prepare a synopsis of events for the daily situation report. To accomplish this, the Watch Officer will maintain a G-3 Journal. Enclosure (1) to TAB E is a sample format of the journal to be used.

    (5) Brief the Air Mission Commander or Flight Leader on supporting fires and air strikes affecting helicopter operations. Brief and coordinate air cavalry and air mobile operations.

    b. The TOC watch will consist of a minimum of three reliefs to permit operation on a 24-hour basis. Watch personnel shall consist of the (1) Training Advisor, (2) Assistant Training Center Advisor, (3) G-2 Advisor. The Artillery Battalion Assistant Advisor for the battalion normally located with the division headquarters shall appear on the watch schedules to assist with preparation of the Division Fire Support Plan.

3. Equipment. Enclosure (2) is a listing of equipment for advisor's support in the FSCC/TOC and is provided from the MAU assets. The G-3 Operations Chief is responsible for procuring and maintaining these items.

4. Displacement Procedures. The procedures for initial displacement of the division for an operation will be in accordance with TAB B to this instruction. Subsequent displacement in continuation of an operation must allow for the uninterrupted command and control of the Division. The Training Advisor will normally travel with the advance element of the FSCC/ROC to assist with establishing the new command post. Communications equipment to be taken forward will depend on the availability of communications equipment and requirements of the individual situation.

5. Helicopter Support. Helicopter requests for all helicopter support (Air Cavalry, Air Mobile, C&C, Admin, Logistics) shall be made in accordance with the format of enclosure (3). The request will be submitted to reach the FSCC by 1800 the preceding day. The OIC FSCC/TOC (Helo LNC) will consolidate the requests and disseminate information on call signs and reporting times after the request is approved. Helicopters will normally be directed to report to the Division FSCC on the ALO frequency and will then be dispatched to the requesting unit. On completion of the mission, the helicopter flight leader should be directed to clear with the Division FSCC (ALO) prior to departing the area. If the Division is operating separate helicopter support zones for the heavy equipment/ammunition lifts and the troops lifts, separate frequencies will be used to control the zones. These frequencies will normally be the Division Command #2 and the Division Airborne Coordinator Net as delineated in TAB C. The unit being resupplied will normally be directed to monitor the appropriate frequency for terminal guidance of the helicopter. Special operations may require more specific instructions for adequate command and control. These procedures will be issued by separate instruction as necessary.

6. Medical Evacuation Request. Medevac requests will be submitted in accordance with the doctrine of the current area of operations. Where feasible, logistics helicopters will be utilized for routine medevac requirements. This decision will be governed by operational requirements and directed from the Division FSCC/TOC.

7. Fixed-Wing Air Support. Fixed wing close air support and B-52 strikes will be preplanned and requested in accordance with directives from higher headquarters. Immediate requests will be requested through the FSCC and will be provided as available. Control of tactical air will normally b exercised by the Airborne FAC.

8. Communications. FSCC/TOC communications will be as indicated in TAB C to this instruction.

STANDING OPERATING PROCEDURES FOR MARINE ADVISORY UNIT

UNIT JOURNAL--G-3 ADVISORY ELEMENT, MARINE ADVISORY UNIT

From:_____

To:_____

TIME	SERIAL #	TIME IN	TIME OUT	INCIDENT	ACTION TAKEN

MISCELLANEOUS NOTES:

LIST OF EQUIPMENT FOR DIVISION FSCC/TOC (INCLUDED IN TAB A)

1. Field Desk (Shared w/G-3 Advisor)

2. Three (3) folding tables or one (1) large table approximately 8' X 10' and one (1) folding table.

3. Five (5) folding chairs.

4. Two (2) map boards 4' X 8' (¼") plywood preferred).

5. Acetate – two (2) rolls clear, one roll frosted.

6. Office supplies including notebooks, writing pads, pencils, paper, clips, pens, file holder, paper punch, accofasteners, thumb tacks, and scissors.

7. China marking pencils, map pin, tape, marking and scotch, and ammo types.

8. Large coffee pot, electric; paper cups.

9. Typewriter (shared with G-3).

10. Two (2) M151 1/4 – ton vehicles w/trailer (normally G-3 and Division Artillery).

11. Two (2) maps of assigned area of operations to include topographic raised relief for Terrain Analysis and Fire Planning.

STANDING OPERATING PROCEDURES FOR MARINE ADVISORY UNIT

HELICOPTER REQUEST

1. Unit_____ Call sign_____

   Frequency_____

2. Type mission_____

3. Number sorties_____

4. Coordinates: Pick-up zone_____

   Landing zone_____

5. Time desire begin mission_____

6. Special instructions_____

_____

_____

CHAPTER XII
GLOSSARY OF TERMS AND ABBREVIATIONS USED IN RVN

ACT	U.S. Air Cavalry Troop
ACTIV	Army Concept Team in Vietnam
AID	Agency for International Development
AIK	Assistance in Kind
ALC	Area Logistical Command
A&L CO	Administrative and Direct Support Logistics Company
ALLADIN	Air Force FAC operating at night using starlight scope and flares to control night air strikes
ANGLICO	Air and Naval Gunfire Liaison Company
APACHE	Call sign of "A" Troop, 7/1 Air Cavalry Squadron (ACS)
ARC LIGHT	Air Force B-52 Strike
ARVN	Army of the Republic of Vietnam
ASPS	Assault Support Patrol Boat
ATC	Armored Troop Carrier (Tango Boat)
ATCO	Air Transportation Coordination Officer
ATSB	Advance Tactical Support Base
A/W	Automatic weapons
AUTUMN MIST	Helicopter defoliation mission utilizing one UH-1 spray aircraft which may or may not be accompanied by a light fire team
BCC	Border Control Centers
BLACK PONY/BRONCO	OV-10 Twin Engine Turboprop Counterinsurgency Aircraft
BLACK HAWK	Call sign of 7/1 Air Cavalry Squadron. It is organized with three air cavalry troops, (ACT) each consisting of 4 LOHs, 4 gunships, 1 Command and Control (C&C) ship and at least 4 troop carrying helos.
BUSHMASTER	An operation conducted by a company-sized unit. The unit inserts into an AO, established a clandestine base of operations, and interdicts enemy LOC and infiltration routes through coordinated platoon sized night ambushes. The duration of the operation various between 24 and 36 hours. Upon completion of the bushmaster, the unit is either extracted or moves by a reconnaissance-in-force to its base camp.

CARE	Co-operation for American Relief Everywhere
CAS	Combined Area Studies
CCB	Command and Communications Boat
CG	Coast Group (VNN)
CHICOM	Chinese Communist
CHIEU HOI	"Open Arms" program which welcomes returnees to the side of the GVN.
CICV	Combined Intelligence Center Vietnam
CIDG	Civilian Irregular Defense Groups – mercenaries of Vietnamese, Laotian, Cambodian descent who fight primarily around own villages.
CMD	Capital Military District
CORDS	Civil Operations Revolutionary Development Support
COMBAT SKYSPOT	High Altitude, radar directed, level flight bombing employing various types of aircraft
COMMACHE	Call sign of "C" Troop, 7/1 Air Cavalry Squadron
CRIP	Civilian Reconnaissance Intelligence Platoon
CRDC	Central Revolutionary Development Council
CRS	Catholic Relief Service
CS	Tear gas grenades
CTZ	Corps Tactical Zone
CZ	Coastal Zone
DELTA HAWK	Call sign of the 255th Aviation Company (Air Surveillance employing OV-1 Mohawk aircraft).
DUFFEL BAG	Acoustical sensors used for surveillance
DUST OFF	Medical evacuation by helicopter
DUTCH MASTER	Call sign of "B" Troop, 7/1 Air Cavalry Squadron (ACS)
DTA	Division Tactical Area
DTZ	Division Tactical Zone
EAGLE FLIGHT	Air cavalry type operation using LOHs, Cobras to initiate contacts followed by helo insertions into contact areas.
EAGLE FLOAT	Troops embarked on river assault craft (RAC) who are inserted when contact is made
ENIFF	Enemy initiated fire fight
FIREFLY	A light fire team (LFT) with a flare or light ship employed in night airfield defense
FSB	Fire Support Base
FWMAF	Free World Military Assistance Forces
GVN	Government of Vietnam

H&I	Harassment and Interdiction Fire Support
HOI CHANH	A Chieu Hoi rallier
HOOK	CH-47 helicopters from an Assault Supply Company (ASHC)
JGS	Joint General Staff (ARVN)
JUSPAO	Joint United States Public Affairs Office
KBAR	A platoon of gunships, one command and control (C&C) ship, and at least 5 troop carrying helicopters available for use by the provinces.
KIA	Killed in action
KIT CARSON SCOUTS	Former Viet Cong who have come over to our side and serve with allied units
LAW	Light anti-tank weapon
LCPL	Landing craft, personnel, large
LUFT	Light fire team (2 helicopter gunships)
LOG	Forward Air Controller Team
LOH	OH-6 Light Observation Helicopter
LRRP	Long Range Reconnaissance Patrol
MACV	Military Assistance Command, Vietnam
MAF	Marine Amphibious Force
MAGPIE	Call sign of Australian B-57 bombers
MAP	Military Assistance Program.
MASF	Military Assistance Service Funded
MEDCAP	Medical Civic Action Program
MINIDUST	Two or more helicopter spray ships accompanied by one or more light fire teams and employed in enemy base areas.
MILCAP	Military Civic Action Program
MINI-PACKAGE	A platoon of gunships, one command and control (C&C) ship, and at least 5 troop carrying helicopters available for use by the provinces.
MONITOR	Heavily armored LCM-6 (40mm cannon, 105mm howitzer or flame gun).
MRB	Mobile Riverine Base
MRF	Mobile Riverine Force
MSB	Mine Sweeper Boat
MSD	Mine Sweeper Drone
NAVLE	Naval Liaison Element
NILO	Naval Intelligence Liaison Officer
NVA	North Vietnames
PADDY CONTROL	Air Force Tactical Radar Control Center for the Delta located at Binh Thuy Air Base

PAT	People's Action Team or Political Action Team
PBR	Patrol Boat River
PCF	Patrol Craft, Fast (SWIFT Boat)
PEGASUS	CH-47 helicopters employed on a standby basis from DMAC TOC to drop bulk CS
PG	Patrol Gunboat
PLATOON OF GUNSHIPS	Two light fire teams (4 helicopter gunships)
PF	Popular force
POLWAR	Political Warfare
PRU	Provincial Reconnaissance Unit
PSA	Provincial Sector Advisor
PSYOPS	Psychological Operations
RAD	River Assault Division
RAG	River Assault Group
RAID	River Assault and Interdiction Division (VNN)
RAS	River Assault Squadron.
RF	Regional Forces
RPG	Rocket Propelled Grenade
RR	Rural Reconstruction
RSSZ	Rung Sat Special Zone
RVNAF	Republic of Vietnam Armed Forces
SAR	Search and Rescue
SEALORDS	South East Asia Land, Ocean, River, Delta Strategy
SEAL	Sea, Air, Land; Special 6 to 8 man Naval Intelligence gathering Detachment
SEAWOLVES	Naval Helicopter Gunships Operating as light or heavy fire teams
SHADOW	C-119 Aircraft with four 7.62mm mini-guns and illumination
SHOTGUN	OI-E Bird-dog observation aircraft from the 221st Reconnaissance Airplane Company (RAC) preassigned to sectors
SLICK	UH-1B Helicopter
SPECTRE	C-130 aircraft with 20mm and 40mm mini-guns, illumination and Infra-red TV for nightobservation support of troops
SPOOKY	C-47 aircraft with four 7.62mm mini-guns and flare illumination capability for night support of troops in contact.
SSB	Swimmer Support Boat (skimmer)
STINGER	C-119K aircraft with 20mm mini-guns and

	illumination use in support of troops with night observation
SVN	South Vietnam
SWING SHIP	UH-1D Helicopter assigned to different sectors or administrative use
TAOR	Tactical Area of Responsibility
TRAIL DUST	Air Force C-123 dispensing defoliant or crop destruction chemical
TSN	Tan Son Nhut
USARV	United States Army, Vietnam
USIS	United States Information Service
USAID	United States Agency for International Development
VC	Viet Cong
VCC	Viet Cong, captured
VCI	Viet Cong Infrastructure
VIS	Vietnamese Information Service
VN	Vietnam or Vietnamese
VNAF	Vietnamese Air Force
VNMC	Vietnamese Marine Corps
VNN	Vietnamese Navy
ZIPPO	Flame thrower equipped ATC or Monitor

U.S. Marine Advisors to the Vietnamese Marine Corps, 1954-1975

Maj Gene A. Adams, Jr.	(70)	Capt David N. Buckner	(72)
Maj Thomas G. Adams	(70)	Maj Talman C. Budd	(67)
Maj Sidney C. Adkins	(71)	Capt Walter J. Buhl	(69)
Capt John H. Admire	(69)	Capt John G. Burke	(63)
GySgt James P. Allen	(70)	1stLt Charles W. Campbell	(69)
Capt Robert C. Allison	(70)	Maj Jack R. Campbell, Jr.	(72)
Capt James A. Amendolia	(70)	Capt Thomas E. Campbell	(67)
Col Nels E. Anderson	(67)	Capt Michael D. Carey	(69)
Capt Peter C. Anderson	(70)	Maj Richard P. Carlisle	(67)
SSgt Robert L. Anderson	(69)	Capt Reid O. Carlock	(72)
Capt James B. Archer	(72)	Capt Gary E. Carlson	(67)
Capt Thomas B. Bagley, Jr.	(68)	Maj Keith E. Carlson	(72)
Capt Russel F. Bailes, Jr.	(72)	Maj Paul L. Carlson	(67)
Capt Duane A. Balfanz	(69)	Capt Marshall N. Carter	(70)
Capt Gerald L. Barlow	(70)	PFC M.T. Carter	(70)
Maj James D. Beans	(72)	Capt Richard M. Cavagnol	(67)
Maj Larned V. Bearce	(70)	Maj Michael D. Cerreta, Jr.	(69)
Capt Lawrence J. Bender II	(70)	Capt Don R. Christensen	(62)
Capt Cecil J. Bennett	(57)	Capt Phillip C. Cisneros	(72)
Capt William F. Bethel	(61)	1stLt Edward B. Clark	(71)
Maj Edward O. Bierman	(70)	Capt William A. Clark, III	(72)
GySgt William C. Bishop	(69)	SSgt R. E. Clemens	(72)
Capt Jerry C. Black	(70)	CWO-3 Jack N. Clow	(73)
Capt Dennis R. Blankenship	(72)	Maj Robert C. Cockell	(71)
GySgt R. G. Bleacher	(70)	Capt Richard V. Coffel	(67)
Capt Bradley W. Bluhm	(70)	Capt William E. Cole, II	(67)
Capt Donald E. Bonsper	(68)	Capt Clelland D. Collins, Jr.	(72)
Maj Walter E. Boomer	(71)	Capt Bernis B. Conaster	(70)
Maj Gerald W. Boston	(72)	LtCol James P. Connolly	(67)
Capt William B. Bovee	(69)	Maj Donald B. Conaty	(70)
Capt Edward H. Boyce	(67)	Col Leroy V. Corbett	(68)
Capt James A. Brabham, Jr.	(71)	GySgt Richard L. Coughlin	(70)
Cmdr C.W. Bramlett (USN)	(70)	Capt Allen M. Coward	(71)
Capt James R. Brandon, III	(67)	SSgt R. R. Crissman	(70)
CWO-3 Shella R. Bray, Jr.	(71)	Maj Alfred J. Croft	(62)
Capt James T. Breckinridge	(55)	LtCol Victor J. Croizat	(56)
Capt Edward E. Bright	(69)	Cpl Bobby G. Crowl	(71)
CWO-3 Ferris D. Brown	(72)	HMC E.E. Currier (USN)	(71)
LtCol Robert E. Brown	(61)	Maj William H. Dabney	(70)

SSgt Elmer C. Daniels	(69)	1stLt Louis Garcia	(67)
SSgt Chester L. Davis	(70)	Capt Phillip E. Gardner	(67)
Capt Donald L. Davis	(69)	Maj Theodore L. Gatchel	(69)
Capt Dale N. Davis	(57)	Capt Lauren W. Gates	(70)
Maj Andrew D. Debona	(71)	Maj Ronald C. Garten	(70)
Capt Godfrey S. Delcuze	(63)	Capt Charles L. George	(70)
Capt Carmine S. Delgrosso	(70)	Maj Umberto Giannelli Jr.	(68)
Capt Thomas R. Delux	(69)	Sgt Ronald A. Glidden	(62)
Capt Chadwick H. Dennis	(67)	Maj Thomas E. Gnibus	(71)
Sgt D.A. Dennisuk	(70)	Maj Charles J. Goode Jr.	(71)
Capt Dennis M. Dickey	(70)	Capt Michael J. Gott	(59)
Capt William M. Dickey	(71)	Capt Herbert M. Gradl	(63)
Capt Gary D. Dockendorf	(72)	GySgt William H. Graeme	(63)
Capt Gunther Dohse	(69)	Capt Samuel T. Gray	(71)
Capt Gustavus L. Donnelly	(70)	Capt William A. Griffis III	(69)
Col Joshua W. Dorsey, III	(71-73)	Capt John S. Grinalds	(67)
Capt George H. Douse	(67)	Capt Roger D. Groot	(67)
Capt James J. Doyle	(70)	Capt Gunnar Gudjonsson	(70)
Capt Thomas V. Draude	(69)	GySgt Robert C. Guilliams	(71)
Capt Marcel J. Dube	(67)	Capt Lyal V. Gustafson	(70)
Maj Peter I. Duggan	(70)	Capt John J. Hainsworth	(67)
SSgt William E. Duncan	(62)	Capt Robert E. Hamilton	(67)
CWO-3 Bobby E. Dusek	(72)	Maj George L. Hammond	(70)
Maj Jon T. Easley	(71)	Maj James E. Harrell	(63)
Capt Clark D. Embrey	(71)	Capt John D. Harrill Jr.	(70)
SSgt Dale L. Eriksson	(69)	Maj Myron C. Harrington, Jr.	(72)
Maj William P. Eshleman	(68)	Capt Ronald C. Harrington	(72)
Capt Robert S. Evasick	(71)	SSgt Clarence R. Harris	(62)
Sgt G. M. Fauteck	(72)	Capt David D. Harris	(72)
LtCol Walter D. Fillmore	(73)	Maj Gene B. Harrison	(70)
Maj Raymond F. Findlay	(72)	Maj William R. Hart	(72)
Capt Alan J. Finger	(69)	Capt Stephen M. Hartnett	(71)
SSgt Robert D. Firman	(71)	SSgt J.W. Harvey	(71)
Maj Robert L. Fischer	(67)	GySgt George M. Hayes	(63)
1stLt William C. Fite III	(68)	Capt William E. Healy	(70)
HMC R.C. Fitzgerald (USN)	(72)	SSgt R. L. Helm	(72)
1stLt Wesley L. Fox	(68)	Capt Thomas W. Hemsath	(67)
CWO-2 George M. Francis	(72)	Maj Porter K. Henderson	(72)
MSgt Milton H. Friedman	(62)	Capt Miguel A. Hernandez	(70)
Capt Dennis B. Fryrear	(67)	Maj Robert A. Hickethier	(70)
GySgt David F. Fureigh	(72)	Maj Jimmie A. Hicks	(67)
Maj Laurence R. Gaboury	(67)	Capt William R. Higgins	(72)
Capt Charles H. Gallina	(73)	CWO-3 James E. Hill	(72)

Lt K. F. Hines (USN)	(68)	Capt Alastair J. Livingston	(72)
Maj Joseph P. Hoar	(67)	Capt Lawrence H. Livingston	(71)
Capt Richard W. Hodory	(72)	GySgt J. C. Lowery	(71)
GySgt Jessie G. Holiday	(67)	GySgt William A. Loyko	(62)
GySgt E.N. Holloway	(70)	LtCol Anthony Lukeman	(74-75)
Capt Terry L. Howard	(72)	Capt Charles A. Lyle	(71)
Maj Emmett S. Huff, Jr.	(71)	Capt Herbert G. Lyles	(70)
Maj Richard D. Hughes	(70)	1stLt Larry S. MacFarlane	(67)
Capt Frank M. Izenour Jr.	(70)	Col John A. MacNeil	(65)
Capt Jack C. James	(70)	Capt William J.P. Mannix	(63)
Capt Robert D. Jassem	(70)	Maj Richard E. Maresco	(70)
HMC J.T. Jenkins (USN)	(69)	Maj David E. Marks	(69)
SSgt C. B Johnson	(62)	Maj Robert J. Martin	(70)
Capt Gilbert D. Johnson	(70)	CWO-2 Travis E. Martin	(68)
Capt James A. Johnson	(69)	Sgt D.L. Mason	(71)
Capt James E. Johnson	(71)	Maj Jon A. Maxwell	(70)
Lt(JG) W. F. Johnson (USN)	(71)	Capt S.F. Mayfield	(69)
Maj Clyde J. Johnston	(72)	Maj William R. McAdams	(72)
Maj Duncan H. Jones	(71)	Capt Gary T. McAlpin	(68)
Capt Richard C. Jones, Jr.	(62)	Capt Peter R. McCarthy	(67)
1stLt Larry Jones	(69)	Capt Jimmy W. McClung	(70)
Capt Walter F. Jones	(72)	Sgt G. J. McDonnell	(63)
Maj James R. Joy	(71)	Maj James R. McElroy, Jr.	(70)
SSgt B. N. Kama	(70)	GySgt Robert L. McElyea	(72)
Capt Cyril L. Kammeier	(68)	Capt Michael J. McGowan	(68)
LtCol Douglas T. Kane	(67)	Maj Robert W. McGowan	(70)
LtCol Raymond H. Kansier	(68)	GySgt R.A. McGuire	(72)
Maj Gordon W. Keiser	(72)	Maj Robert C. McInteer	(72)
Maj Robert D. Kelley	(71)	Maj William E. McKinstry	(68)
Maj William M. Keys	(72)	Maj Paul A. McLaughlin	(72)
Capt Charles W. King	(71)	LtCol Alexander P. McMillan	(70)
Capt Harold P. Klunk	(70)	Lt R. E. McPeters (USN)	(70)
Capt Donald E. Koepler	(63)	Capt Frederick C. McQuigg	(71)
Capt Earl A. Kruger	(72)	Capt James P. McWilliams Jr.	(63)
Capt J.L. Kuyendall (USA)	(68)	Capt Eric W. Mezger	(72)
Capt Raymond Labas	(62)	Col Richard L. Michael, Jr.	(67)
Capt John J. Lacy	(71)	Cpl C. J. Miller	(71)
1stLt James L. Laney	(67)	Maj John G. Miller	(70)
Sgt R.R. Langdon	(71)	Capt Charles P Minor, III	(72)
Maj William G. Leftwich, Jr.	(65)	GySgt Ado Mobley, Jr.	(67)
Capt Stephen E. Lindblom	(70)	LtCol Clarence G. Moody Jr.	(62)
1stLt Allen A. Lindeman	(67)	Capt William S. Moriarty	(67)
Capt Steven P. Lindsey	(71)	Capt Peter S. Morosoff	(72)

GySgt James A. Morris	(71)	Capt Nelson P. Ralph	(69)
1stLt James J. Mortimer, Jr.	(70)	Capt Leon C. Ramsey	(71)
Maj John J. Mullen, Jr.	(69)	Capt David S. Randall	(71)
Capt John D. Murray	(71)	Capt Philip H. Ray	(70)
Capt James M. Myatt	(70)	Capt Ronald D. Ray	(67)
Capt Richard I. Neal	(70)	Capt Joseph C. Raymond	(69)
Col William P. Nesbit	(64)	Capt Charles L. Redding	(72)
Capt Allen D. Nettleingham	(71)	Capt Robert K. Redlin	(72)
2dLt Melvin P. Neu	(70)	Capt Henry L. Reed	(70)
1stLt Keith M. Nolan	(71)	Capt Richard M. Reilly	(69)
LtCol Wesley C. Noren	(63)	Capt Ronald R. Rice	(71)
Capt Phillip C. Norton	(71)	Maj Jon A. Kindfleisch	(68)
Maj Joseph J. O'Brien	(72)	Capt John W. Ripley	(71)
Maj Martin E. O'Connor	(69)	Maj Ernest G. Rivers	(70)
Maj John W. O'Donnell	(67)	Capt Lewis C. Roberts	(69)
Capt Jermone X. O'Donovan Jr.	(72)	LtCol Clifford J. Robichaud, Jr.	(60)
Lt Roger J. Oldham (USN)	(71)	Capt Joe D. Robinson	(72)
HMI Waitman L. Orr (USN)	(67)	GySgt T.M. Robinson	(62)
Capt Richard R. Osterberg	(69)	LtCol Glen W. Rodney	(67)
Capt Thomas F. O'Tolle, Jr.	(71)	Capt Jeffrey T. Ronald	(72)
Maj S. E. Otts [?]	(70)	Maj Geoffrey H. Root	(71)
Capt Robert A. Packard Jr.	(72)	Maj Richard B. Rothwell	(72)
Maj Charles E. Parker	(67)	GySgt R. L. Rouse	(62)
Capt Evan L. Parker, Jr.	(62)	Capt Morris E. Ruddick Jr.	(69)
LtCol Tom D. Parsons	(69)	Capt Manfred E. Schwarz	(67)
GySgt C. D. Peck	(63)	Capt James W. Seal	(72)
2dLt Walter A. Peeples	(67)	2dLt William H. Sexton	(67)
Capt James P. Perkins	(69)	Capt Merlyn A. Sexton	(71)
Capt Frank G. Perrin	(56)	Lt P. R. Shackleford (USN)	(69)
Capt Jack N. Perrin	(69)	Capt Harry J. Shane	(68)
1stLt Richard P. Perry	(68)	Capt John J. Sheehan	(68)
Capt George Phillip III	(71)	SSgt B.S. Sheldon	(69)
Maj John Pipta	(72)	Capt Roy H. Shelton, Jr.	(69)
Sgt C. L. Pitchford	(72)	Maj Robert F. Sheridan	(71)
LtCol James A. Poland	(71)	Maj Robert D. Shoptaw	(72)
WO-1 W. T. Pope	(72)	Capt Jerry I. Simpson	(67)
Capt Richard L. Porter	(69)	Maj Cloyce E. Sinclair	(70)
Maj Stanley G. Pratt	(71)	HMC G. D. Smith (USN)	(70)
CWO Joseph W. E. Pratte	(68)	Capt Gordon F. Smith	(69)
Maj Donald L. Price	(71)	Capt Joseph N. Smith	(63)
SSgt P.A. Prusak	(71)	Capt Michael W. Smith	(69)
Maj Donald C. Pease	(72)	Capt Richard L. Smith	(71)
Sgt M.L. Rallsback	(63)	Capt Bradley S. Snell	(61)

Capt John T. Somerville	(68)	1stLt William C. Ward	(71)
Capt William J. Spangler	(72)	Capt Philip J. Walsh	(70)
Capt V.M. Stalankiewicz	(70)	Maj William R. Warren	(71)
Capt John C. Sternberg, Jr.	(69)	Capt Jerome L. Weis	(70)
Capt John E. Stocking	(69)	GySgt P. B. Wells	(70)
LtCol George E. Strickland	(73-74)	Capt Marshal R. Wells	(70)
Maj William C. Stroup	(70)	Maj Oliver M. Whipple Jr.	(71)
GySgt J. C. Sturges	(69)	1stLt Carlton P. White	(68)
GySgt B. J. Sturzl	(72)	LtCol Michael E. White	(69)
Maj James R. Sweeney	(72)	1stLt Robert L. Whited	(67)
Maj William T. Sweeney	(71	MSgt R. A. Wichman	(62)
LtCol William G. Swigert	(71)	Capt Jonathan W. Wilbor	(72)
GySgt J. Sykora Jr.	(72)	Capt Gary Wilder	(58)
Capt William P. Symolon	(71)	LtCol Frank R. Wilkinson Jr.	(60)
Capt Jack K. Taylor	(70)	LtCol William N. Wilkes	(56)
Capt Richard B. Taylor	(62)	Capt J. A. Williams	(68)
Capt Thomas C. Taylor	(68)	Capt James R. Williams	(70)
Capt John W. Theisen	(72)	Capt Robert O. Wills	(70)
GySgt A. E. Thompson	(70)	SSgt C. J. Wilson	(62)
Col Francis W. Tief	(70)	Capt William D. Wischmeyer	(71)
Sgt G. L. Toal	(69)	SSgt W. D. Wiscarver	(72)
Maj Frederic L. Tolleson	(70)	Maj Donald E. Wood	(67)
Maj James M. Tully	(72)	GySgt L. W. Woods	(63)
LtCol Gerald H. Turley	(72)	GySgt Lance P. Woodburn	(69)
Capt James Sterling G. Turner	(60)	GySgt C. Wright, Jr.	(67)
Capt James F. Vaillancourt	(57)	Maj Regan R. Wright	(71)
Capt Willem Vanhemert	(63)	Capt Thomas Zalewski	(72)
Capt James K. VanRiper	(67)	Capt J. L. Zellers	(71)
Col William M. VanZuyen	(69)	Capt Frank Zimolzak	(62)
1stLt R.V. Visesti	(70)	1stLt Anthony C. Zinni	(67)
Maj Harold T. Ward Jr.	(68)		

Note: List according to Senior Marine Advisor, 0073: wdw, 5750, 22 March 1973.

Further Reading

LtCol Thomas D. Affourtit. *Analysis of a Culture in Conflict: Comparative Personality Determinants between U.S. Marine Advisors and Vietnamese Soldiers.* U.S. Marine Advisory Publications, n.d. http://www.irism.com/pubs/

LtCol Thomas D. Affourtit. *Communion in Conflict: The Marine Advisor, Vietnam, 1954-1973.* U.S. Marine Advisory Publications, 1975. http://www.irism.com/pubs/

LtCol Thomas D. Affourtit. *USMC Covan (Vietnam) Survey.* U.S. Marine Advisory Publications, n.d. http://www.irism.com/pubs/

GySgt Tom Bartlett. "Captain Cool," *Leatherneck*, November 1966, pp. 36-41.

GySgt Tom Bartlett. "Vietnamese Marines," *Leatherneck*, December 1966, pp. 28-31.

LtCol Donald E. Bonsper. "Combat Memoir," *Marine Corps Gazette*, February 1986, pp. 22-25; March 1986, pp. 22-23; April 1986, pp. 45-46; June 1986, pp. 27-29; July 1986, pp. 17-19; August 1986, pp. 16-17; September 1986, p. 23.

Maj Tom Campbell. "Ambush at Song O Lau," *Marine Corps Gazette*, January 1970, pp. 35-36.

Col Victor J. Croizat. "Origin of the Vietnamese Marine Corps, *Marine Corps Gazette*, December 1970, p. 14.

Col Victor J. Croizat. "Starting the Corps in South Vietnam," *Naval History*, March/April 1996, pp. 45-49.

Col Victor J. Croizat. "Vietnamese Naval Forces: Origin of the Species," *U.S. Naval Institute Proceedings*, February 1973, pp. 48-58.

"For the Marines." Vietnamese Marine website, http://tqlcvn.org/english/descend.html

LtCol Douglas T. Kane. "Vietnamese Marines in Joint Operations," *Military Review*, November 1968, pp. 26-33.

LtCol Paul X. Kelly. "Ambush and Reaction," *Infantry in Vietnam*. Ft Benning,

Ga.: Infantry Journal, 1967, pp. 74-80.

MajGen L. Nguyen Khang. "Republic of Vietnam Marine Corps," *Marine Corps Gazette*, November 1966, pp. 65-68.

LtCol William G. Leftwich, Jr. "And a Few Marines," *U.S. Naval Institute Proceedings*, August 1968, pp. 34-45.

LtCol William G. Leftwich, Jr. "Bong Son Operation," *Marine Corps Gazette*, June 1966, pp. 29-31.

LtCol William G. Leftwich, Jr. "Decision at Duc Co," *Marine Corps Gazette*, February 1967, pp. 35-38.

"Marines: Vietnamese Marine Corps," *Leatherneck*, November 1963, p. 43.

CSM Michael N. Martin, USA. *Warriors of the Sea: Marines of the Second Indochina War*. Paducah, Ky.: Turner Publishing, 2001.

Maj Charles D. Melson. "In Their Own Image: The Battle for Quang Tri, South Vietnam, and the Deployment of the Vietnamese Marine Division," paper, Society for Military History/Royal Military College, May 1993.

Maj Charles D. Melson. "The Vietnamese Marine Corps—VNMC," *Fortitudine*, Vol. 33, No. 1, 2008, pp. 9-13.

Maj Charles D. Melson. "Tiger Stripes and Green Berets," *Military History Illustrated*, September 1993, pp. 20-26.

Maj Charles D. Melson. *Vietnam Marines, 1965-1973*. Oxford, UK: Osprey Publishing, 1992.

Col John G. Miller. "Born in Battle," *The Marines*. Harrisburg, Pa.: NHS Publications, 1989, pp. 123-29.

Col John G. Miller. *The Bridge at Dong Ha*. Annapolis, Md.: Naval Institute Press, 1989.

Col John G. Miller. *The Co-Vans: U.S. Marine Advisors in Vietnam*. Annapolis, Md.: Naval Institute Press, 2000.

Maj Nguyen Thanh Tri. "Vietnamese Advisor," *Marine Corps Gazette*, December 1968, pp. 29-32.

LtCol Gerald H. Turley and Maj Marshall R. Wells. "Easter Invasion, 1972," *Marine Corps Gazette*, March 1973, pp. 18-29.

LtCol Gerald H. Turley. *The Easter Offensive*. Novato, Ca.: Presidio Press, 1985.

U.S. Marine Corps, various authors. *U.S. Marines in Vietnam* official history series. Washington, D.C.: History and Museums Division, 1977-1997.

Oral Histories

Maj Larned V. Bearce. Period Covered: 1970. Transcript. Marine Corps University GRC Archives, Quantico, Va.

Maj Edward O. Bierman. Period Covered: 1970. Recording. Marine Corps University GRC Archives, Quantico, Va.

Maj Walter E. Boomer.[i] Period covered: 1971. Transcript. Marine Corps University GRC Archives, Quantico, Va.

Capt James T. Breckinridge. Period covered: 1955. Recording. Marine Corps University GRC Archives, Quantico, Va.

Maj Robert C. Cockell. Period covered: 1971. Transcript. Marine Corps University GRC Archives, Quantico, Va.

Col Leroy V. Corbett. Period covered: 1968. Recording. Marine Corps University GRC GRC Archives, Quantico, Va.

LtCol Victor J. Croizat. Period covered: 1956. Transcript. Marine Corps University GRC Archives, Quantico, Va.

Maj William H. Dabney. Period covered: 1970. Transcript. Marine Corps University GRCArchives, Quantico, Va.

Maj Andrew D. Debona. Period covered: 1971. Transcript. Marine Corps University GRC Archives, Quantico, Va.

Capt James J. Doyle. Period covered: 1970. Transcript. Marine Corps University GRC Archives, Quantico, Va.

1stLt William C. Fite. Period covered: 1968. Transcript. Marine Corps University GRC Archives, Quantico, Va.

Capt Dennis B. Fryrear. Period covered: 1967. Recording. Marine Corps University GRC Archives, Quantico, Va.

Maj Thomas E. Gnibus.[ii] Period covered: 1971. Recording. Marine Corps University GRC Archives, Quantico, Va.

Capt John S. Grinalds. Period covered: 1967. Transcript. Marine Corps University GRC Archives, Quantico, Va.

Maj Joseph P. Hoar. Period covered: 1967. Recording. Marine Corps University GRC Archives, Quantico, Va.

Capt James E. Johnson. Period covered: 1971. Transcript. Marine Corps University GRC Archives, Quantico, Va.

Capt Lawrence H. Livingston. Period covered: 1971. Transcript. Marine Corps University GRC Archives, Quantico, Va.

LtCol Anthony Lukeman. Period covered: 1974. Transcript. Marine Corps University GRC Archives, Quantico, Va.

Capt Frederick C. McQuigg. Period covered: 1971. Recording. Marine Corps University GRC Archives, Quantico, Va.

Col Richard L. Michael. Period covered: 1967. Recording. Marine Corps University GRC Archives, Quantico, Va.

Capt James M. Myatt. Period covered: 1970. Transcript. Marine Corps University GRC Archives, Quantico, Va.

Capt Richard I. Neal. Period covered: 1970. Transcript. Marine Corps University GRC Archives, Quantico, Va.

Capt Allen D. Nettleingham. Period covered: 1971. Transcript. Marine Corps University GRC Archives, Quantico, Va.

Capt George Philip, III.[iii] Period covered: 1971. Recording. Marine Corps University GRC Archives, Quantico, Va.

Maj Donald L. Price. Period covered: 1971. Recording. Marine Corps University GRC Archives, Quantico, Va.

Capt John W. Ripley. Period covered: 1971. Transcript. Marine Corps University GRC Archives, Quantico, Va.

Maj Robert F. Sheridan. Period covered: 1971. Transcript. Marine Corps University GRC Archives, Quantico, Va.

Capt Richard L. Smith.[iv] Period covered: 1969. Transcript. Marine Corps University GRC Archives, Quantico, Va.

LtCol Gerald H. Turley. Period covered: 1972. Transcript. Marine Corps University GRC Archives, Quantico, Va.

Maj William R. Warren.[v] Period covered: 1971. Transcript. Marine Corps University GRC Archives, Quantico, Va.

Capt Gary Wilder.[vi] Period covered: 1958. Transcript. Marine Corps University GRC Archives, Quantico, Va.

LtCol Frank R. Wilkinson, Jr. Period covered: 1960. Transcript. Marine Corps University GRC Archives, Quantico, Va.

Capt William D. Wischmeyer.[vii] Period covered: 1971. Transcript. Marine Corps University GRC Archives, Quantico, Va.

GySgt Levi W. Woods. Period covered: 1963. Recording. Marine Corps University GRC Archives, Quantico, Va.

Maj Regan R. Wright. Period covered: 1971. Transcript. Marine Corps University GRC Archives, Quantico, Va.

1stLt Anthony C. Zinni. Period covered: 1967. Transcript. Marine Corps University GRC Archives, Quantico, Va.

---

[i] Interviewed with Capt R.L. Smith.
[ii] Interviewed with Capt G. Philip, III.
[iii] Interviewed with Maj T.E. Gnibus.
[iv] Interviewed with Maj W.E. Boomer.
[v] Interviewed with Capt W.D. Wischmeyer.
[vi] There is more than one interview with this individual.
[vii] Interviewed with Maj W.R. Warren.

188

Back Cover: The logotype reproduced on the back cover has as its major element the oldest military insignia in continuous use in the United States. It first appeared, as shown here, on Marine Corps buttons adopted in 1804. With the stars changed to five points, the device has continued on Marine Corps buttons to the present day.

www.ingramcontent.com/pod-product-compliance
Lightning Source LLC
Chambersburg PA
CBHW080505110426
42742CB00017B/3003